M000194987

Alterity and Transcendence

European Perspectives

European Perspectives
A Series in Social Thought and Cultural Criticism
Lawrence D. Kritzman, Editor

European Perspectives presents outstanding books by leading
European thinkers. With both classic and contemporary works,
the series aims to shape the major intellectual controversies of
our day and to facilitate the tasks of historical understanding.

A complete series list follows the index.

Alterity and Transcendence

EMMANUEL LEVINAS

Translated by Michael B. Smith

COLUMBIA UNIVERSITY PRESS
NEW YORK

Columbia University Press
Publishers Since 1893
New York
Copyright © Columbia University Press 1999
All rights reserved

First published in the United Kingdom in 1999 by
THE ATHLONE PRESS
1 Park Drive, London NW11 7SG

Originally published as *Altérité et Transcendence* © 1995 Fata
Morgana

The publishers wish to express their appreciation of assistance given
by the government of France through Le Ministère de la Culture in
the preparation of this translation.

Library of Congress Cataloging-in-Publication Data

Levinas, Emmanuel.
    [Altérité et transcendence.   English]
    Alterity and transcendence / Emmanuel Levinas ; translated by
Michael B. Smith.
        p.   cm.
    Includes bibliographical references and index.
    ISBN 978-0-231-11651-0 (pbk. : alk. paper)
    1. Transcendence (Philosophy)   I. Title.
B2430.L483A4813   1999
194—dc21   98-47784
                                                                CIP

Contents

Contents

Translator's Note

The French 'moi' is consistently translated as *I*, and the French 'je' as I, without the italics. The pronoun 'he' and related forms are sometimes used, as in the French original, to refer to hypothetical persons of either sex; the terms 'man' and 'fellow man' are also used in this way. Levinas's 'prochain,' a nominalized adjective meaning 'next,' is translated sometimes as 'fellow man' and sometimes as 'neighbour.'

English words in square brackets, if in the main text, are intended to clarify ambiguities in my translation; if in the footnotes, to differentiate my notes from those of the author. Italicized French words in brackets are Levinas's own, which I supply either in cases in which a technical distinction might otherwise be lost, or when the morphology of the original word carries semantic connotations that cannot be translated.

I would like to express my gratitude to Alisa Ray of the Berry College Faculty Research and Sponsored Programs Office for final manuscript preparation, and to my wife Helen for her helpful stylistic suggestions.

Preface

Philosophy Between Totality and Transcendence

by Pierre Hayat

'Philosophy is Platonic'
(Emmanuel Levinas)

'Alterity and Transcendence' the title Emmanuel Levinas has chosen for the present volume, which groups twelve texts written between 1967 and 1989, leads us directly to the idea that transcendence is 'alive in the relation to the other man' (see below, p. 126).

How are we to perceive what is at stake in this thesis of Levinas's? First, by recalling that 'transcendence' can be construed variously. Levinas insists that etymologically 'transcendence indicates a movement of crossing over (*trans*), but also of ascent (*scando*).'[1] In its etymological sense, transcendence leads us to the notion of going beyond, of upward movement, or of a gesture that moves beyond itself. Transcendence would appear to be the marker of the paradox of a relation with what is separate. 'It is a way for the distant to give itself.'

This tension toward the beyond – this look lifted toward the heights – would, on this view, originally be mediated through the sacred. Human beings bowed before what was beyond them. Their greatness came from their being dissolved into a higher domain of being, that of the absolute or eternal.

Such is clearly not the direction taken by Levinas. For in that figure of transcendence we recognize the 'magic mentality' that prompts men to believe that the world in which they live is governed by mysterious powers. Levinas reminds us that Western philosophy has contributed to the liberation of men from that 'false and cruel transcendence.'[2] Reason delivers us from the illusion of a 'world-behind-the-world.' It frees mankind from the fear of an imaginary beyond. The world that, having become for man an object of knowledge, has lost its troubling strangeness, henceforth appears without secrets and open to theoretical investigation and within technology's grasp.

Does this mean that today transcendence has lost all meaning? With the modern philosophies of the subject, we are witnessing a transmutation of the idea of transcendence, rather than its eviction. Transcendence cannot be reduced to the transcendent. It does not define a dimension of the real that reaches beyond the inner life. It accompanies the birth of human subjectivity. 'It is not a question here of making transcendence subjective, but of being amazed at subjectivity (...) as the very *modality* of the metaphysical.'[3]

Thus, man is no longer required to dissolve into a higher reality. Transcendence becomes the intimate structure of subjectivity. In other words, it is subjectivity that is found at the beginning of the movement of transcendence. Levinas calls upon Jean Wahl, his friend and interlocutor for several decades, to express that idea. 'Man is always beyond himself. But that beyond-oneself must eventually be conscious of the fact that it is himself that is the source of transcendence.'[4] The transcendence of subjectivity attests to this amazing possibility of going beyond any actual situation and exceeding any definition.

But 'modern philosophy,' looking at transcendence from the point of view of subjectivity, renders the notion of transcendence problematic. Indeed, is there not something like an an antinomy in the proposition: 'The subject transcends itself'? Either we have a true transcendence, but in that case the subject is carried along in its transcendent movement, and, in that adventure, the subject, ceasing to be itself, loses its identity, or its substance; or the subject remains itself in its movement of transcendence, but then there may be doubt as to whether or not there is true transcendence.[5] Thus, 'the celebrated *project* of the modern philosophers, in which the subject surpasses itself by creating,' returns the subject to itself, without making a true transcendence, a going out from self, possible.[6]

What is the source of this impossibility, for the modern philosopher, of maintaining the subject intact in the movement of transcendence, without the latter's losing its meaning? It lies in his persistant attachment to the age-old privilege of the One. Whether transcendence expresses the subject's ability to distance itself from any real actuality and affirm itself as pure freedom, or whether it refers to the subject's power of realizing itself in history through its works, its underlying principle is in the idea of the identity of being.

Levinas is dedicated to rethinking transcendence by other pathways than those taken by the modern philosophies of the subject. To do this, he does not give a definition of transcendence *a priori*, but shows how a 'new transcendence' is the very meaning of 'the human.' Levinas's philosophy is constructed on the basis of a non-constructed intuition: that of the upsurge of transcendence as a '*question* to the Other and about the other.'[7] Transcendence is born of the intersubjective relation.

But in order to bring transcendence into view does it suffice to assent to the foundational character of intersubjectivity? When the intersubjective relation is presented as a mirror-like relation in which each subject stands face to face with the freedom of the other, alterity is still being thought on the basis of the identity of the *I*. Transcendence, or the going out from oneself, cannot, under these circumstances, come into view. *A fortiori*, the desire for recognition does not bring a true transcendence into the subject, since through the other it is itself that the subject is seeking.

In such a relational context, conflict ineluctably becomes the essential mode of the relation to the other, as each subject sees its power of transcendence wrested from it by the other. And as Sartre writes: 'The other as a look is nothing but this: my transcendence transcended.'[8]

In order for a true transcendence to be possible, the other must concern the *I*, while at the same time remaining external to it. It is especially necessary that the other, by his very exeriority, his alterity, should cause the *I* to exit the self. Levinas wants to show that the other, by his face, attests to himself, simply, directly, without going through any mediation. That exceptional capacity of the face to testify to itself outside all objective context and independently of the intersubjective field is, of itself, a message addressed to the subject. By the non-ordinary manner in which it manifests itself, the face opposes violence with metaphysical resistance. In doing so, the face raises the subject to responsibility.

We see how Levinas proposes to think the intersubjective relation: not as a reciprocal but as a asymmetrical relation; not on the basis of a common space but across the *écart* separating the *I* from the other, as a lowering, in discontinuity.

In such a relation, the *I* does not put itself in question; it is put in question by the other. It is precisely in taking the other as one's point of departure that transcendence can emerge. True transcendence is not born of the interiority of a being, of which it would be the prolongation or idealization, but of exteriority. Transcendence cannot, consequently, be felt otherwise than as a subjectivity in crisis, that finds itself facing the other, whom it can neither contain nor take up, and who nonetheless puts it in question.

The face of the other is the locus of transcendence in that it calls into question the *I* in its existence as a being for itself. There is in this something like a trauma of transcendence that prevents the *I* from remaining within itself, and carries it to the limits of itself. But in that accusation of the *I* by the other, human subjectivity as responsible for the other and before the other is formed. Levinas's philosophy rehabilitates pluralism, setting out from the interhuman face-to-face that cannot be resolved into a higher unity. But pluralism first defines the structure of subjectivity. The *I* paradoxically finds within itself 'the other as such,' that will never be interior to itself.

The first text of this volume sheds particular light on the way Levinas understands transcendence. The study 'Philosophy and Transcendence' (1989), published in the *Encyclopédie Philosophique Universelle*, is exemplary of the way a great philosopher can inscribe his own approach in his relation to other philosophers. Levinas examines the way Plotinus, Descartes, Husserl and Heidegger have encountered the question of transcendence, showing how the search for the original locus of transcendence 'is doubtless one of the main problems of philosophy' (p. 4). But Levinas also shows that through the question of transcendence it is philosophy itself that is called into question. For in the amazement that prompts philosophical questioning Levinas recognizes the 'disproportion between *cogitatio* and *cogitatum*' that attests to transcendence (p. 3).

The manner in which Levinas presents the Plotinian approach is significant in this regard. 'The transcendence of the One' in Plotinus expresses the philosophical awakening itself, understood as 'the aspiration to a wisdom that is not knowledge, that is not representation, that is love' (p. 8). That *élan* toward the One attests, in Levinas's view, to a certain way of philosophizing that makes of philosophy the privileged mode of expression of a nostalgic desire for fusion. Such a philosophy, which associates transcendence and the search for unity, fails to recognize 'the idea of an effective transcendence in sociality' (*ibid.*). Here Levinas shows his opposition to the 'philosophies of the same' – he, the philosopher who recognizes in the relation to the human face the original locus of transcendence. Through transcendence, Levinas's pluralist philosophy desires to do justice to the irreducible exteriority of the face and the ultimate plurality of the interhuman relation.

*

Setting out from transcendence, we are thus led to two cardinal categories of Levinas's philosophy: totality and infinity. Two articles published in the *Encyclopaedia Universalis*, 'Totalité et totalisation' and 'Infini,' have the virtue of both proposing a precise conceptual analysis of these two categories and of outlining how the main currents of Western philosophy have approached them.

These two articles in the *Encyclopaedia Universalis* seem to me to be of particular interest for an understanding of Levinas's philosophy. Levinas's readers know the use he makes of the idea of the infinite in Descartes, and are not unaware of the presence of Rosenzweig in inspiring his critical examination of the idea of totality. But in the two studies reproduced here, Levinas also shows how the pre-Socratics, Aristotle, Leibniz, Spinoza and Kant deal with the ideas of totality and the infinite.

Levinas's intent is obviously not to present a compilation of reference works. Like 'Philosophy and Transcendence,' the articles 'Totality and Totalization' and 'The Infinite,' testify to the deep immersion of Levinas's thought in the history of philosophy, and to his taking up of a position that is affirmed within that history. Here we are led into Levinas's 'laboratory,' in which the author of *Totality and Infinity* confronts the procedures of the great metaphysical systems with his own, on the basis of a theoretical and historical elaboration of the notions of totality and infinity. As such, these two texts may be read as a response, perhaps, to the reproach that Levinas makes an overly personal, and slightly equivocal use of the categories of totality and infinity.

It has been suggested, in particular, that Levinas's

definition of the totality as a unity possessing an intrinsic reality and proceeding from an exclusive principle is 'reductionist.' May not Levinas have imprudently enlisted in the polemic conducted by Franz Rosenzweig against philosophers 'from Ionia to Jena,' taking up the view that totality would not leave room for the particularity of beings? Thus, for example, can one not conceive of a living organism as a totality without thereby reducing it to an abstract generality? For the idea of a biological totality allows one precisely to show what makes up the concrete reality of a singular being. Not only does the idea of totality not necessarily lead us to think that reality is homogeneous (the parts of a whole can themselves be diverse), it reveals the diversity of reality differently, according to whether the totality is static or dynamic, and whether its parts define the elements of a structure or the phases of an evolution.

The article 'Totality and Totalization,' a unique text in the Levinas corpus, is the occasion for reminding us that the idea of totality is, in the history of philosophy, the object of a variety of approaches. The totality designates the perceptual synthesis, but also the unity of the concept and the unconditionality of the regulative idea. Levinas also emphasizes that the totality is at the heart of philosophical reflection on the truth defined as a totality, on history understood as totalization, and yet again on the hermeneutic method that intertwines the whole and the part. It therefore seems that this study should not be over-

looked by anyone wishing to grasp the value of
Levinas's critique of the totality.

That critique is primarily directed at the postulate
underlying thoughts of totality: the totality leaves
nothing outside (p. 41). Such a postulate applies in the
first instance to thought, to the extent that totality
gathers the diversity of reality into a sole concept. But
it also applies to society, since the social totality makes
possible the grouping of individuals in the same place,
beneath the same set of laws and amidst the same
institutions.

It is in taking the idea of the infinite as his starting
point that Levinas justifies the overflowing of the
totality, since there is no common measure between
the idea of the infinite and the infinite of which it is
the idea. The thought of the infinite does not take
possession of the infinite of which it is the idea.
Setting out from the infinite, which 'is close to the
idea of transcendence,' ethical responsibility is vali-
dated (p. 54). That responsibility of the *I* is brought
about by the other man, who is refractory to concep-
tualization, and whose social status does not do justice
to his uniqueness. Thus we see that the refusal of
totality does not derive, in Levinas, from a decree of
the *I*, but rather from the relation to the face, which
'blocks totalization.'

Does this mean that Levinas asks us to chose the
infinite over the totality? That would be a misunderstanding. Ethical transcendence wrests the individual
free from the social totality, but is reflected within

the totality itself when it is a question of assuring the coexistence of responsibility for the other and the equality of all before the law.

Just as ethical responsibility is not unaware of the social totality, so thought could not constitute itself without the work of the concept. Between the totality and the infinite, Levinas's philosophy lets a tension, rather than a disjunction, appear. It affirms the primacy of ethics, which exceeds but does not exclude the concept.

Between the concept and the infinite, between totality and transcendence, Levinas's philosophy traces a singular path, one that runs into that of the masters of Western philosophy. Levinas reminds us that in Plato truth is the result of the synthesis of the concept, but that the good is to be sought beyond being, in an impossible totalization (p. 50). Can we not discern here a double homage to Platonic philosophy – to a conceptual, clear and universalizable philosophy, but also to a philosophy open to transcendence, beyond totality?

*

Just as transcendence is not a philosophical theme among others because it calls philosophy itself into question, so ethics is not, in Levinas, a branch of philosophy, because it is given as 'first philosophy.' The relation to the other who addresses the *I* is, for Levinas, the ultimate situation, or the 'last presupposition.' Question of the question, source of all questions: the relation to the other forbids philosophical discourse from closing in upon itself. It is from this angle that Levinas wonders about the dialogical essence of philosophy.

Four texts included here – 'Beyond Dialogue' (1967), 'The Word I, the Word You, the Word God' (1978), 'Ethics and First Philosophy. Proximity to the Other' (1986), and the preface to Martin Buber's *Utopie et socialisme* (1977)[9] – show how the occasion of dialogue allows Levinas to validate the primacy of ethics.

Already in Plato it is shown that philosophy is not to be reduced to the *logos* because it implies the relation with an interlocutor. The quest for truth cannot be detached from the living presence of the interlocutors. But the Platonic dialogue has as its goal the union of the participants in the dialogue around the true idea.[10]

The merit of Martin Buber's philosophy of dialogue is precisely that it brings out the intrinsic value of the dialogical I-Thou relation. 'Buber's thought prompted me to engage in a phenomenology of sociality' (p. 103). Buber teaches us that relation between the I who addresses a thou and the thou who calls upon an *I* is the initial structure of meaning, beyond what can be stated. In the text of 1978, published on the occasion of the 100th anniversary of Buber's birth, Levinas writes: 'To say "you" is the primary fact of Saying . . . Saying is that rectitude from me to you, that directness of the face-to-face, directness of the encounter' par excellence (p. 93).

This text, which presents a wonderful homage to the philosophy of Martin Buber, allows us to nuance the interpretations that merely oppose Levinas to Buber, forgetting the deep ties that bind the two thinkers.

But Levinas also initiates a difficult dialogue with Buber. When Levinas declares, 'When I speak of first philosophy, I am referring to a philosophy of dialogue that cannot not be an ethics,' we recognize a proximity to Buber: the beginning of philosophy is not the ← *cogito*, but the relation to the other (p. 98). But we also understand that Levinas diverges from Buber by recognizing in the dialogue the non-reversible circumstance of ethics.

Thus, the originary dialogue is situated 'beyond the dialogue' in that it testifies to 'the search for a proximity beyond the ideas exchanged, a proximity that lasts even after dialogue has become impossible' (p. 87). That the fundamental conjuncture of the human is not the agreement of men around shared ideas Buber had perceived. But for Levinas the relation that constantly reinstates the humanity of man is not the formal structure of the reciprocal relation in which the I is a you for the other and the you is discovered to be another I. Beyond the reversibility of that structure, Levinas wants to find the asymmetrical ethical relation, which consists for the *I* in 'going toward the Other where he is truly other' (p. 88).[11]

Levinas continues to pursue this dialogue with Buber in the preface to *Utopie et socialisme*. After having presented Buber's thesis, which sets the political and the social in opposition to one another, Levinas inquires into the possiblity of socialism's appearing 'as a new ethics' (p. 116). That 'utopian' dimension of human sociality is, in Buber, thematized in the model of the 'I and Thou,' on the basis of which a social relation without powers could be conceived (p. 117). But with Levinas 'the utopia of the human,' which means that the meaning of the human is never closed up in a place, is to be sought in the asymmetrical relation between the other man and me.

*

The ethical transcendence that springs up in the interpersonal relation indicates that the egalitarian and reciprocal relation is not the ultimate structure of the human. So it is that the infinity of the face of the other man is the living refutation of the pretension of the social totality, the economic and administrative structure, to be sufficient unto itself. Three texts – 'The Prohibition Against Representation and "the Rights of Man"' (1984), 'Peace and Proximity' (1984), and 'The Rights of the Other Man' (1989) – attest to that preoccupation of Levinas's, by initiating a discussion on rights and peace.

Levinas reminds the reader that the 'rights of man' are *a priori* in that they are affirmed independently of 'all agreed upon law' (p. 145). But he also stresses that they become effective when they are 'incorporated into the judicial determinism' by taking root in a State (*ibid.*). Thus the notion of right includes both the reality of positive laws and the idea in the name of which men have the 'task' of 'formulating the requirements of freedom' (p. 147). But a right is always the expression of the agreement of wills surrounding the law. It is the 'free limitation (of freedom) in consenting to the rationality of the universal' (*ibid.*).

Levinas's effort consists in producing a critique of the thought of the rights of man. That critique is not an external questioning of the philosophy of the rights of man, but rather a quest for its conditions of possibility. In that journey toward the ultimate source of the right, Levinas finds the individual responsibility of man before the other man: '*The rights of man, absolutely and originally*, take on meaning only in the other, as the right of the other man. A right with respect to which I am never released' (p. 127)[12].

This statement of Levinas's could be misunderstood if we failed to emphasize its problematic nature. For the 'right of the other man' is not an abstraction: it does not take on meaning 'in thin air,' in forgetfulness of human society. It has already been emphasized that the transcendence of the infinite is reflected in the social totality. One may also recall that statement in *Totality and Infinity*, doubtless one of the strongest and most difficult of that work: 'The third party looks at me from the eyes of the other person,' which means that all the others are 'present' in the face-to-face.[13]

So it is that the non-egalitarian and interpersonal structure of the ethical relation, the very one that transcends the political order, is corrected by the requirement of equality that comes from the taking into account of the third party. The same ambiguity is found regarding the right: The affirmation of the right of the other man subverts the general idea of the rights of man but carries within it the solicitude for the rights of all mankind.

Two conversations open out this work of Levinas, for whom 'philosophy is never wisdom, because the interlocutor it has just embraced has already escaped.'[14] The first conversation, with Christian Chabanis, concerns death (1982). In the second, Levinas responds to the questions of Angelo Bianchi (1985).

The section titles are by Pierre Hayat, who thanks Monsieur Michaël Levinas for his discreet and invaluable assistance.

I

THE OTHER TRANSCENDENCE

1

Philosophy and Transcendence

I
THE IDEA OF INFINITY

Ten years ago, I wrote: 'The transcendence of things in relation to the lived intimacy of thought – in relation to thought as *Erlebnis*, in relation to the lived (which is not fully expressed by the idea of a "still confused" and non-objectifying consciousness) – the transcendence of the object, of an environment, like the ideality of a thematized notion, is opened, but is also traversed, by intentionality. It signifies distance as much as it does accessibility. It is a way for the distant to be given. *Perception* already grasps; the concept – *the Begriff* – retains that sense of seizure. Whatever effort may be required for the appropriation and utilization of things and notions, their transcendence promises possession and enjoyment that consecrates the lived adequation of thought to its object in thought, the identification of the Same, satisfaction. Astonishment – a disproportion between *cogitatio* and *cogitatum* – in which knowledge is in pursuit of itself, is dulled in knowledge. This way for the real to exist in intentional transcendence "on the same scale" as the lived, and for thought to think on its scale and thus to enjoy, is what is meant by immanence.¹' An awakening of thought to knowledge, to presence, to being; to re-presentation, to knowledge, to the secret will that wills and intends in the intention, reversing the latter in an act of constitution. Is that the original awakening of thought? Had it not already been opened to a deeper vigilance, to which is revealed, beyond all *unveiling*, that which cannot be contained in any representation? A transcendence of the Cartesian idea of the Infinite, in a thinking that finds itself thinking more than it can embrace, the blinding bedazzlement of the gaze by an excess of light and a bursting of knowledge in adoration – to which Descartes alludes at the end of the Third Meditation. Beyond the objective, which is always already correlative to a prior 'aim' and intention to discover – behold an other that *reveals itself*, but that does so precisely in surprising the intentions of subjective thought and eluding the form of the look, totalitarian as presence – eluding the transcendental synthesis. An exceptional idea of the Infinite that has escaped being, and of a presence stronger and more venerable than the totality. An idea that cannot, by virtue of the 'ontological argument,' be peremptorily relegated to presence, to being that is locked within the totalizing look, nor to some other world, nor some empty heaven.

The search for the original locus of that idea of the Infinite and its transcendence is doubtless one of the main problems of philosophy. A locus to be sought in the dimensions of the humanity of man. Drunk with being *in himself* and *for himself* in the presence – or the modernity – that he unveils by his cognitive thought and more indubitably planted in his *cogito* than his feet on the ground, man is capable of sobering up and of dis-interestedness and extreme vigilance *vis-à-vis* his absolutely other fellow man. A vigilance that is not that of the look. The vigilance of a responsibility that – from me to the other, irreducible – concerns me *qua* chosen and irreplaceable, and thus unique and unique only thus, in that identity of I, above all form, outside every order, whom the work of the transcendental constitution already presupposes. Is not the face of one's fellow man the original locus in which transcendence calls an authority with a silent voice in which God comes to the mind? Original locus of the Infinite. Dimension of alterity and transcendence, which we shall speak more of at the end of this reflection, after having insisted upon the ecstatic and metaphysical transcendence taught by the Greeks, its transformation into a philosophy of immanence in which the transcendental structures absorb the exigencies of the absolute, but in which the *I* even of the 'I think' that supports them has not yet clarified its identity of the unique one.

II
THE TRANSCENDENCE OF THE ONE

For Plotinus (*Enneades* V, 1, 6), thought as the act of knowing or intellection, in the duality of *seeing* and *seen*, emanated from the transcendence of the *One*, from its unity or repose, untroubled by any relation of multiplicity, not even that of self-consciousness, which would already be knowledge and duality. The emanation itself is called 'movement of the Immobile,' a contradiction in the order of knowledge! Already in Plato's *Parmenides*, the *One* refused to give itself up to any of the possibilities, any of the hypotheses of a thought that remained knowledge, i.e. thematization and presence of being; it refused to give itself up without even constructing itself dialectically with respect to that question, without formulating itself as thinkable on the basis of the negations of its refusal, be it only to take on the substantive form in which it is evoked in the Platonic dialogue.

The intellection that has emanated from the One, the intellection *of* the One is, by its very thematization, already multiple. But not only because of the distance that separates the intellection from the intelligible. As distant from the *One*, its only dealings would be with a multiplicity of 'Platonic ideas' instead of having *in act* to do with the One, with which, in the form of an outline, it had to do *in potentia*. A strange circumstance in the intellection of the One.

It does indeed think this principle, but in trying to grasp it in its simplicity, it diverges from it and takes into itself other things, which multiply. . . . It possessed a vague outline of the object of its vision, without which it would not have received it into itself, but that object, from being one, has become many; it is thus that it knows it in order to see it and has become vision in act.[2]

It has already missed, or fails to grasp, the unity of the One as it attains, in act, ideas. But the intellection that is intellection of the multiple ideas is not separated from the One absolutely by that multiplicity, which remains nostalgia for the One, homesickness. That which might be called the movement of knowledge – seeing – (or, in today's terminology, the noetic-noematic intentionality of knowledge) filled but dispersed, is, precisely by virtue of its dispersion, a state of privation, compared to the unity of the One. And yet, as if the One were *sensed* in that very privation, as if knowledge, still aspiration by the fact of the dispersion of its seeing, went *beyond* what it sees and thematizes and were precisely thereby a *transcendence*; by the very deficiency of its plural rationality; as if its dispersed accession to multiple being [*essence*] were a piety – Plotinus speaks of *prayer*[3] – with respect to the inaccessible One. Ambiguity, or risk incurred by being at a distance from the One in the knowledge of the intelligence, in the

7

intelligible, the multiplicity of which may keep one far from the 'fatherland,' but thus, as privation, 'hollowed out,' attach one to it. Just as at the next, lower level of emanation, the *soul*, separated from the intelligence and dispersing itself among the things of this world, is capable of gathering itself and prepares to 'hear the voices from on high.' This 'gathering of itself,' this 'turning back to oneself' this knowledge that in the consciousness of self is already an aspiring to higher than self, to the intelligible of intelligence and from there to the One.

This nostalgia, or this piety or gathering of oneself, going beyond and above the intelligible that is present to the intelligence – is philosophy, aspiration to a wisdom, that is not knowledge, that is not representation, that is love. Love of a wisdom other than the intelligible giving itself to knowledge. Philosophy that would thus be transcendence itself. Philosophy as union with the One or fusion with it, inscribing itself in an ecstatic itinerary the steps of which we cannot retrace here. It begins in any case in the intelligence, though the latter is transcended in its privation of the One. Transcendence toward the One with which union is possible. It seems to me important to recognize the attention given in the School of Plotinus to the instants of accomplishment effectively attained by the master: the union with the One is not a utopian ideal. It is not love as aspiration that is triumphant transcendence, but love as union. The idea of an effective transcendence in sociality itself, in proximity

8

rather than in ecstasy, will remain foreign to Greek thought. Let us note the classicism of that thought that, through neo-Platonism, was transmitted to Western philosophy, making it impossible for philosophy not to recognize, down to the time of Hegel, the dissatisfaction in aspiration. Already the notion of the unhappy consciousness! All complacency in dissatisfaction (and even in love as aspiration) under the pretext that they contain, 'hollowed out,' what they lack – all renunciation of wisdom in favor of the simple love of wisdom, or philosophy, would one day come to be looked upon as romanticism, a pejorative appellation. Philosophy, always dissatisfied with being just philosophy! The return to the One of that which was dispersed from it without diminishing it – the coinciding with the source of the 'beyond being' – was to be the big question, in the separation of the intelligence from the One, for the philosophy that emerged from it. The aspiration *to return* is the very breath of the Spirit; but the consummate unity with the One, a pure identity in which all multiplicity and all number are abolished in the rare 'instants' attested to by Plotinus, when distance, or even the distinction of knowledge – be it only the distinction between knowing and the known in the consciousness of self – disappears without leaving any traces. The One to which intelligence piously aspires, beyond the ideas it attains and grasps in their multiplicity (in which, however, it is completed, realized, in act, satis-fied) – the One beyond the noema that is equaled by the noesis of intelligence – would be, according to the neo-Platonic schema, better than that aspiration and that approach from which the One is still absent. There is love in the look of knowing, but, because of that absence which is again signified by the dispersal of the known, that love is worthwhile only because of the transcendent immobility it seeks and in which the seeking is absorbed, because of the One in which the lover coincides with the loved without distinction, in which the movement of ecstasy is abolished and forgotten. The consummate unity of the One, a 'satiety of Kronos'[4] for all eternity is worth more than love, still subject to time, and that, in Plato's *Symposium*, according to the teaching of Diotima, remains a demigod.

III
THE TRANSCENDENCE OF KNOWLEDGE AND THE PHILOSOPHY OF IMMANENCE

Neo-Platonism, exalting that consummate unity beyond being and knowing, better than being and knowing, offered the monotheism that conquered Europe in the first centuries of our era an itinerary and stations capable of corresponding to mystical tastes and the needs of salvation. Piety could be understood as modeling itself on the activity of the intelligence, on its vision in act of a multiplicity of ideas, a vision that did not actualize its 'outline *in potentia,*' its 'project of the One,' but was 'attached, relatively' to it, by its very privation. 'Prayer' expressed the metaphor of that relation, of that presence by absence, in the ascendancy of the thought of knowledge and Intelligence. Knowledge as presence, as being and beings – a multiplicity of ideas, to be sure, but also their gathering together, their synthesis, their understanding, their compresence in the unity of their apperception, in which temporal dispersion passes for a privation of intelligibility that is recuperated in re-presentation or ideality – vision dominating the process of becoming. The evolution of Western thought, freeing itself from the transcendence of the One, but finding it again in the unity of the system and the immanence of transcendental unity. The return in immanence – in the world that is perceived, embraced, mine – of the very large and quasi-formal structures of the neo-Platonic schemata, the contours of which can still be clearly discerned in the set of modern Hegelian or Husserlian themes. These structures mark <u>the return of transcendent thought to itself</u>, the identity of the identical and the non-identical in self-consciousness, which recognizes itself as infinite thought '<u>without other</u>' in Hegel. And, on another plane, they command Husserl's 'phenomenological reduction,' in which the identity of pure consciousness carries within itself, in the guise of the 'I think,' understood as <u>intentionality</u> – *ego cogito cogitatum* – all 'transcendence,' all alterity. 'All externality' reduces to or returns to the immanence of a

11

subjectivity that itself and in itself exteriorizes itself. The first person of the present in the *cogito*, in which Hegel and Husserl find themselves standing on the ground of modern philosophy, guarantees knowledge its congenital synthesizing and its self-sufficiency, foreshadowing the systematic unity of consciousness, and the integration of all that is *other* into the system and the present, or the synchrony (or the a-temporal) of the system. This is a set of philosophical themes in which time is subordinated to eternity, to a present that does not pass – nor is there any getting beyond it in the universal and eidetic laws governing the empirical dispersion in the a-temporal ideality that stands, immobile, above the immediate temporality of human patience, in the substitution of dialectical rigor for the 'incompressible,' indispensable *durée* that must not be ignored. Or else time is subordinated to eternity in accordance with another intention and project, when the 'phenomenological description' ventures behind or beneath abstraction, ideality or the formal structure of speculative time. Does not Husserl's analysis of time come down to expressing time in terms of presence and simultaneity – of retained or anticipated presents? Temporal sciences! As if time were reducible to its way of making itself known, or its manner of conforming to the requirements of its manifestation. An analysis in which the meaning of the meaningful would be equivalent to its aptness to the present and representation, to the simultaneity of a manifold entering into and unfolding within a theme; or, more radically yet, its aptness to *presence*, i.e., to being (taken in its verbal sense). As if, in the notion of presence – or in the notion of being expressed by presence – a privileged mode of time were fused with the birth of knowledge itself, in representation, thematization and intentionality. As if knowledge, concreteness of presence, were the psychism of all thought. Manifestation, in this way of thinking, would coincide with the signifying of meaning and appeal to understanding. Representation (*Vergegenwärtigung*) – memory and imagination – would wrest from the past and the future (simple modes of misunderstanding, of inaccessibility to the hand, and thus of the incomprehensible) a presence, already or still ungraspable, of the past or the yet to come. Representation would be the first grasp of it, to which the intellect refers back, for the *comprehension* it founds. It would bring these 'presents,' at first ungraspable, of the past and future, to the simultaneity of the theme. As if time, in its diachrony came down to a failed eternity, to 'the moving image of an immobile eternity,' or of the consummate One. Henri Bergson, who, for the first time in the history of ideas, attempts to conceive time outside that failure of eternity, has characterized the destiny of that notion in philosophy as that of a becoming that passes for a privation of eternity.

The rationality of knowledge would correspond to the absolute of the One. Knowledge rejoining, here below – in the immanence of the obvious manifestation – the known of being, or rejoining, in reflection, the transcendental concreteness of oneself, is fulfilled or accomplished: *wird erfüllt*. The equality of the One to itself – a supposedly prototypical equality – has thus become, in knowledge, adequation, and, from there, satis-faction and as such, as the very signifying of the meaningful, the secret of a civilization. Knowledge as research is still privation, but it is no longer a powerless and pious nostalgia for the transcendence of the unattainable – or only in exceptional circumstances attained – One. The presence of being in truth is grasp and appropriation, and knowledge is a teleological activity. What remains in thought *'in potentia'* is also a power. A teleology animates consciousness, according to Husserl's *Crisis*.[5] Consciousness moves toward an end, a terminus, a given, a world. Knowledge is intentionality: act and will. An *auf etwas hinauswollen* [desire to get somewhere], an 'I want' and an 'I can' that the term intention itself suggests. An 'I want' and an 'I represent to myself' that Husserl at least takes as being included in intentionality. A thought that un-thinks itself in order to represent or master presence. Being in its presence offers itself to a taking in hand; it is donation. The most abstract lessons of science begin in a world that we inhabit, amidst things that are within hand's reach. These are things given in a world that is given that Husserl calls 'life-world.' The intentionality of consciousness is concretely grasp, perception and concept, praxis incarnate in all knowledge, the precocious

14

promise of its technical prolongations and of consumption. The being that is correlative to consciousness, already signifying on the basis of an ontology that could be called idealist, is datum and donation and *to be taken*. The meaning of satis-faction does not just come down to the abstract adequation of a perceived matching a perception. The concreteness of satisfaction is enjoyment. A 'lived' that is not simply a 'content of consciousness,' but that is *signifying*: in it the identity of the 'I am,' of the *cogito* content with itself and persevering in its being, is identified. Identification of the free ipseity of Western man within the limits of his powers.

A freedom that only obstacles can limit: natural and social forces, and death. The obstacles of nature and society, over which knowledge can progressively triumph. The obstacle of death the unassumable, the incomprehensible, which accredits the idea of a 'finite freedom.'

But freedom is always measured by its powers. The marvel of Western man in his modernity, which is probably essential to him: the ideal of the satisfied man to whom all the possible is permitted.

The questions that we have to ask can now be formulated. Does thought only think as besiegement of all alterity, disappearing in the unity of the result or in the identity of the identical and the non-identical, engulfing the absolute affected or extinguished in it, in the ambiguity of philosophical idealism or realism? Does thought thinking the absolute signify nothing but need, lack and nostalgia or satisfaction, accomplishment and enjoyment? Does the diachrony of time signify only deficiency of presence and nostalgia? Cannot thought approach the absolute otherwise than by knowledge and in knowledge and excel by that approach, better than the return to the One and coincidence with unity? It is to the dominant conception of traditional philosophy, according to which thought is fundamentally knowledge, i.e., intentionality – will and representation – that some limits are to be delineated. My analysis will take as its point of departure some reflections on the intentional act.

IV
THE RELATIONSHIP TO THE OTHER MAN

I begin with intentionality as set forth in Husserl's phenomenology. In it, the equivalence between thought and knowledge in its relation to being is formulated in the most direct way. While isolating the idea of an original, non-theoretical intentionality from the affective and active life of the soul, Husserl appears to have kept as its basis the representation – the objectifying act – adopting on this point Brentano's thesis, despite all the precautions he took with his new formulation of that thesis. Now, knowledge is, in itself, a relation to something other than consciousness and, as it were, the aim or the willing of that other, which is its object. Husserl, in examining the intentionality of consciousness, wishes to determine '*worauf sie eigentlich hinauswill*' [what it is, essentially, that it wants to get at]. That will, already suggested by the word intention, suggests and justifies the use of the term 'acts' to designate the units of consciousness. In the intuition of truth, knowledge is described as a fulfilling, as the satisfying of an aspiration toward the object. A grasping of being equivalent to the constitution of that being: the transcendental reduction, in suspending all independence in being other than that of consciousness itself, allows us to recover that being suspended as noema or noesis and leads us – or is supposed to lead us – to the full consciousness of self affirming itself as absolute being, confirming itself as an *I* who identifies himself through all the differences, 'Master of himself, just as he is master of the universe,'[6] and capable of shedding light in all the shadowy corners in which that mastery of the *I* would be contested. If the constituting *I* runs up against a sphere in which he finds himself bodily intertwined with what he constituted, he is there in the world as if in his skin, in accordance with the intimacy of the incarnation that no longer has the exteriority of the objective world.

But a reduced consciousness – which, in reflection on itself rejoins and masters, like objects in the world, its own acts of perception and knowledge, and thus confirms self-consciousness and absolute being – also remains, as if supplementarily, non-intentional consciousness of itself, without any voluntary aim; non-intentional consciousness acting as knowledge, unbeknownst to itself, of the active *I* that represents the world and objects to itself. It accompanies all the intentional processes of the consciousness of the *I* that, in that consciousness 'acts' and 'wants' and has intentions. A consciousness of consciousness, 'indirect' and implicit, without any initiative proceeding from an *I*, without aim. A consciousness that is passive, like the time that passes and ages me without me. An immediate consciousness of self, non-intentional, to be distinguished from reflection, from inner perception to which the non-intentional would be apt to become the inner object, or which reflection would be tempted to replace in order to render explicit its latent messages.

The intentional consciousness of reflection, taking the transcendental *I*, its states and mental acts, as its object, can also thematize and seize or explicate all of its non-intentional lived experience, qualified as implicit. It is invited to do so by philosophy in its fundamental project, which consists in bringing to light the inevitable transcendental naiveté of a consciousness forgetful of its horizons, of its implicit elements and the time it lasts.

Hence one is prompted – too quickly no doubt – to consider in philosophy all that immediate consciousness solely as non-explicit knowledge, or as a still confused representation to be brought to full light. This would be the obscure context of the thematized world that reflection, intentional consciousness, will convert to clear and distinct data, like those that present the perceived world itself or absolute reduced consciousness.

Still, we have the right to ask whether the non-intentional, which is lived in the margin of the intentional, retains and delivers up its true meaning when subjected to the scrutiny of reflective consciousness. The critique traditionally directed against introspection has always suspected a modification that 'spontaneous' consciousness would undergo beneath the scrutinizing, thematizing, objectifying and indiscreet eye of reflection – a kind of violation and lack of recognition of a certain secret. An ever refuted, ever renewed critique.

I ask: What goes on in that non-reflective consciousness that is taken to be only pre-reflective, and that, implicit, accompanies intentional consciousness, which in reflection aims intentionally at the thinking self, as if the thinking *I* appeared in the world and belonged there? What can that supposed confusion, that implication, mean positively, so to speak?

Does the 'knowledge' of pre-reflective self-consciousness know how to talk, properly speaking? A confused consciousness, an implicit consciousness preceding all intention – or *durée* having gotten over all intention – it is not an act but pure passivity. Not only by virtue of its *being-without-having-chosen-to-be*, or by virtue of its fall into a tangle of possibilities already realized before all voluntary taking up, as in

Heidegger's *Geworfenheit* [thrownness]. A 'consciousness' that rather than signifying a knowledge of self is a self-effacement or discretion of presence. Pure *durée* of time that the phenomenological analysis describes, nonetheless, in reflection, as structured intentionally according to an interplay of retentions and protentions that, in the *durée* of time itself, remain at least inexplicit; a *durée* removed from all will of the *I*, absolutely outside the activity of the *I*, and that, as aging, is probably the actual carrying out of the *passive* synthesis on the basis of the passivity of the *lapse* whose irreversibility no act of memory, reconstituting the past, can reverse. The temporality of time escaping *a limine* [from the threshold] by virtue of its lapse, all activity of representation. Does not the implication of the implicit signify *otherwise*, here, than as does knowledge that has been taken away, otherwise than a way of envisioning the presence or non-presence of the future and the past? *Durée* as pure *durée*, as non-intervention, as being-without-insistence, as being-on tiptoe, as being without daring to be: instance of the instant without the insistence of the *I*, and already a lapse, that 'leaves while entering'! A bad conscience, that implication of the non-intentional: without intentions, without aims, without the protective mask of the individual [*personnage*] contemplating himself in the mirror of the world, reassured and striking a pose. Without name, situation or titles. A presence that dreads presence, that dreads the insistence of the identical *I*, stripped

20

of all attributes. In his non-intentionality, on the
hither side of all willing, before any fault, in its non-
intentional identification, the identity backs away
before its affirmation, is worried before what the
return to self of identification may have in the way of
insistence. Bad conscience or timidity; without culpa-
bility, but accused; and responsible for its very presence. The reserve of the non-invested, the
non-justified, the 'stranger on the earth' according to
the expression of the psalmist, of the stateless person
or the 'homeless' who dares not enter. The interiority
of the mental – perhaps that is what it is originally:
that lack of boldness to affirm oneself in being and in
one's skin. Not being-in-the-world, but being-in-question. In reference to which, in memory of which, the
I that already posits itself and affirms itself – or firms
itself up – in being, remains sufficiently ambiguous –
or sufficiently enigmatic – to recognize itself as being,
according to Pascal's formulation, hateful in the very
manifestation of its emphatic identity as an ipseity, in
the 'saying I.' The superb priority of A is A, the
principle of intelligibility, that sovereignty, that freedom in the human *I*, is also, if one may express it so,
the occurrence of humility. A putting into question
of the affirmation and firming up of being, that is
echoed in the celebrated – and easily rhetorical –
quest for the 'meaning of life,' as if the absolute *I* that
has already taken on meaning on the basis of the
psychic or social vital forces, or of its transcendental
sovereignty, went back to its bad conscience.

21

Pre-reflective, non-intentional consciousness cannot become conscious of that passivity; as if, in it, already there was the distinction between the reflection of a subject positing itself in the 'indeclinable nominative,' assured of its perfect right to be and 'dominating' the timidity of the non-intentional, like a childhood of the mind to be gotten over, like an access of weakness in an impassible psyche. The non-intentional is passivity from the start, the accusative is its 'first case,' so to speak. A bad conscience that is not the finiteness of existing signified in anguish. My death, always premature, may check the being that *qua* being perseveres in its being, but in anguish, this scandal does not shake the good conscience of being, nor the morals based on the inalienable right of the *conatus*, which is also the right and the good conscience of freedom. On the other hand, in the passivity of the non-intentional – in the very mode of its 'spontaneity' and before all formulation of metaphysical ideas on this subject – the very justice of being posited in being *is put in question*; being, that is affirmed with intentional thought, knowledge and the grasping of the now. Here we have being as bad conscience, in that putting in question; being-in-question, but also put before the question. Having to answer. The birth of language in responsibility. Having to speak, having to say *I*, being in the first person. Being me, precisely; but from then on, in the affirmation of its being me, having to answer for its right to be. Pascal's 'the *I* is hateful' must be thought through to this point.

To have to answer for one's right to be, not in relation to the abstraction of some anonymous law, some legal entity, but in fear for the other. My being-in-the-world or my 'place in the sun,' my home – have they not been the usurpation of places belonging to others already oppressed by me or starved, expelled to a Third World: rejecting, excluding, exiling, despoiling, killing. 'My place in the sun,' said Pascal, 'the beginning and the archetype of the usurpation of the entire world.'[7] Fear for all that my existence – despite its intentional and conscious innocence – can accomplish in the way of violence and murder. Fear coming from behind my 'self-consciousness' and whatever returns there may be of the pure perseverance in being toward good conscience. Fear of occupying in the *Da* of my *Dasein* someone else's place; the inability to have a place, a profound utopia.[8] Fear that comes to me from the face of the other.

I have already spoken much about the face of the other as being the original locus of the meaningful. May I be permitted to return for a moment to the description of the irruption of the face in the phenomenal order of appearance?

The proximity of the other is the signifying of the face. A signifying that is immediately from beyond the plastic forms that keep covering it up like a mask with their presence in perception. Incessantly it penetrates these forms. Before any particular expression – and beneath all particular expression that, already pose and countenance given to itself, covers and

23

protects it – there is the nakedness and baring of expression as such, i.e., extreme exposure, no defense, vulnerability itself. Extreme exposure, before all human aim – as in a 'point blank' shot. Extradition of the besieged and the hunted – of the hunted before any hunt and any battue. Face in its directness of facing . . ., directness of exposure to invisible death, to a mysterious forlornness. Mortality – beyond the visibility of the unveiled – and prior to all knowledge of death. An expression that tempts and guides the violence of the first crime: its homicidal directness is already singularly well adjusted in its aim at the exposure or the expression of the face. The first murderer may not know the result of the blow he is about to deliver, but his aim of violence makes him find the line through which death reaches the face of the other with undeflectable directness; traced out as the trajectory of the blow delivered and the arrow that kills.

But that face facing me, in its expression – in its mortality – summons me, demands me, requires me: as if the invisible death faced by the face of the other – pure alterity, separate, somehow, from any whole – were 'my business.' As if, unknown by the other whom already, in the nakedness of his face, it concerns, it 'regarded me' before its confrontation with me, before being the death that stares me, myself, in the face. The death of the other man puts me on the spot, calls me into question, as if I, by my possible indifference, became the accomplice of that death, invisible to the other who is exposed to it; and as if, even before being condemned to it myself, I had to answer for that death of the other, and not leave the other alone to his deathly solitude. It is precisely in that recalling of me to my responsibility by the face that summons me, that demands me, that requires me – it is in that calling into question – that the other is my neighbour.

That way of requiring me, of putting me in question and appealing to me, to my responsibility for the death of the other, is a meaning so irreducible that it is on that basis that the meaning of death must be understood, beyond the abstract dialectic of being and its negation, to which, on the basis of violence that has been reduced to negation and annihilation, one reduces[9] death. Death signifies in the concretization[10] of what is for me the impossible abandonment of the other to his solitude, in the prohibition addressed to me regarding that abandonment. Its meaning begins in the interhuman. Death signifies primordially in the proximity of the other man itself or in sociality; just as it is on the basis of the face of the other that the commandment by which God comes to my mind is signified[11] to me.

Fear for the other, fear for the death of the other man, is my fear, but in no way similar to being frightened.[12] Thus it departs from the admirable phenomenological analysis that *Sein und Zeit* [Being and Time] proposes of affectivity, or *Befindlichkeit*: a reflexive structure expressed in a pronominal verb, in which emotion is always the emotion *of* something that moves us, but also emotion for oneself; in which emotion consists in being moved [*s'émouvoir*] – in being frightened *of* something, elated *about* something, saddened *because of* something, but it also consists in being elating for oneself [*se réjouir pour soi*], in being saddened for oneself, etc. I am troubled and worried about my death. A double intentionality of *of* and *for*, and thus a return to oneself, a return to the anguish for oneself, to anguish for one's finitude: in the fear of the dog, an anguish for my death. The fear for the other man does not return to being anguish for my death. It overflows the ontology of Heidegger's *Dasein* and his good conscience of being with respect to that being itself. There is an ethical awakening and vigilance in this affective disturbance. Heidegger's being-toward-death marks, indeed, for *a being*, the end of his being-with-respect-to-that-being-itself, and the scandal of that end, but in that end no scruple about being awakens.

V

ETHICAL TRANSCENDENCE AND PHILOSOPHY

In the naturalness of being-with-respect-to-that-being-itself, in relation to which all things – and even the other man – seem to take on meaning, essential nature is called into question. A turning on the basis of the face of the other, in which, at the very heart of

the phenomenon, in its very light, a surplus of significance is signified that could be designated as glory. It
demands me, requires me, summons me. Should we
not call this demand or this interpellation or this
summons to responsibility the word of God? Does
not God come to the mind precisely in that summons,
rather than in the thematization of the thinkable,
rather even than in some invitation to dialogue? Does
not that summons to responsibility destroy the forms
of generality in which my store of knowledge, my
knowledge of the other man, represents the latter to
me as similar to me, designating me instead in the
face of the other as responsible with no possible
denial, and thus, as the unique and chosen one?

The orientation of consciousness toward being in
its ontological perseverance or its being-toward-death,
in which consciousness is certain it is going to the
ultimate – all that is interrupted before the face of
the other man. It is perhaps that beyond being and
death that the word glory, to which I had recourse in
speaking of the face, signifies.

The human behind perseverance in being! Behind
the affirmation of being persisting analytically – or
animally – in its being, and in which the ideal vigor
of the identity that identifies itself and affirms itself
and fortifies itself in the life of individual human
beings and in their struggle for vital existence, conscious or unconscious and rational – the wonder of
the *I* vindicated in the face of the other, is also like
the suspension (like the *epochē*) of the eternal and

27

irreversible return of the identical to itself, and of the inviolability of its logical and ontological privilege. Suspension of its ideal priority, which negates all alterity by murder or by engulfing and totalizing thought. Suspension of war and politics that contrive to pass for the relations of the Same to the Other. In the *I*'s deposition of its *I*-sovereignty, in the modality of the hateful *I*, the ethical but also probably the spirituality of the soul itself, and certainly the question of the meaning of being, i.e. its call for justification, is signified. It signifies – through the ambiguity of the identical that says *I* to itself at the height of its unconditional and even logically indiscernible identity, autonomy above all criteria; but that can, precisely at that height of unconditional identity, confess to its being the hateful *I*.

The *I* is the very crisis of the being of a being [*l'être de l'étant*] in the human. A crisis of being, not because the meaning of this verb (in its semantic secret) remains to be understood and is an appeal to ontology, but because, being myself, I already ask myself whether my being is justified, whether the *Da* of my *Dasein* is not already the usurpation of someone's place.

Bad conscience that comes to me from the face of the other, who, in his mortality, tears me from the solid ground on which I, a simple individual, place myself and persevere naively, naturally, in my position. Bad conscience that puts me in question. A question that does not await a theoretical response in the form of information. A question that appeals to responsibility, which is not a practical last resort, offering consolation for the failure of knowledge, incapable of equaling being.

A responsibility that is not the privation of the knowledge that comprehends and grasps, but the excellence of ethical proximity in its sociality, in its love without concupiscence.

The human is the return to the interiority of non-intentional consciousness, to bad conscience, to the possibility of its fearing injustice more than death, of preferring injustice suffered to injustice committed, and what justifies being to what ensures it.

VI
THE TIME OF TRANSCENDENCE

I have attempted to carry out a phenomenology of sociality, starting out from the face of the other man, reading, before all mimicry, in its facial directness, a defenseless exposure to the mysterious forlornness of death, and hearing, before all verbal expression, from the bottom of that weakness, a voice that commands, an order issued [*signifié*] to me not to remain indifferent to that death, not to let the other die alone, i.e., to answer for the life of the other man, at the risk of becoming the accomplice of that death. The other's facing, in its directness, would appear to signify both the defenselessness and the opposition of alterity, an authority that is missing in the simply logical alterity,

29

which identifies individuals and concepts and distinguishes them from one another, or, opposes notions to one another by contradiction or contrariety. The alterity of the other is the extreme point of 'Thou shalt not commit homicide,' and, in me, fear for all the violence and usurpation my existence, despite its intentional innocence, risks committing. The risk of occupying, from the moment of the *Da* of *Dasein*, the place of another, and thus, concretely, of exiling him, of condemning him to a miserable condition in some 'Third' or 'Fourth' World, of killing him. Thus there emerges, from that fear for the other man, an unlimited responsibility, one that we are never discharged of, one that does not end in the last extremity of the neighbour, even if the responsibility then only amounts to responding, in the powerless confrontation with the death of the other, 'Here I am.' A responsibility that harbors the secret of sociality, the total gratuitousness of which, though it be ultimately in vain, is called the love of one's neighbour, love without concupiscence, but as irrefrangible as death.

Sociality, not to be confused with some weakness or privation in the unity of the One. From the depths of natural perseverance in the being of a being who is assured of his right to be, from the heart of the original identity of the *I* – and against that perseverance, and against that identity – there arises, awakened before the face of the other, a responsibility for the other to whom I was committed *before* any committing, before being present to myself or coming back to self.

What does this *before* mean? Is it the before of an *a priori*? But would it not in that case come down to the priority of an idea that in the 'deep past' of innateness was already a present correlative to the *I think*, and that − retained, conserved, or resuscitated in the duration of time, in temporality taken as the flow of instants − would be, by memory, re-presented? By that route, the privilege of the present would be maintained; the present, the sovereign expression of which is Plato's theory of reminiscence. Thus a reference of thought to perception would be assured. And thus the privilege or transcendence of eternity would be assured, as that of a present-that-does-not-pass, in the ideality of the idea; an eternity whose *durée* or diachrony of time would be only dissimulation or deformation or privation in man's finite consciousness. Also the privilege of the *I think*, 'stronger' than time, and gathering the scattered temporal shadows into the unity of transcendental apperception, the firmest and most formal of forms, stronger than any heterogeneity of contents − to identify the diversity of experience, in embracing and seizing it again, *qua* identified, in the knowledge of being, into which it enters. Fragments of the ancient, unique One, regained. The *I* or the *I think* that identifies would be the reason and *logos* of rationality. Ontology would henceforth be interpreted not just as a knowledge that duplicates being, but as the ultimate return of the identity of being to itself, as a return to the One.

It is, on the contrary, a past irreducible to the present that seems to signify in the ethical anteriority of responsibility-for-the-other, without reference to my identity assured of its right. Here I am, in that responsibility cast back toward something that was never my fault, never my doing, toward something that was never in my power, nor my freedom – toward something that does not come back to me from memory. Ethical significance of a past that concerns me, that 'regards me,' that is 'my business' outside all reminiscence, all retention, all representation, all reference to a remembered present. Significance in the ethics of a pure past, irreducible to my present, and thus, of an originary past. Originary significance of an immemorial past, based on responsibility for the other man. My non-intentional participation in the history of humanity, in the past of others, who are my business.

The responsibility for the other is not reducible to a thought going back to an idea given in the past to the 'I think' and rediscovered by it. The natural *conatus essendi* of a sovereign *I* is put in question before the face of the other, in the ethical vigilance in which the sovereignty of the *I* recognizes itself as 'hateful,' and its place in the sun 'the prototype and beginning of the usurpation of the whole earth.' The responsibility for the other *signified* – as an order – in the face of the neighbour is not in me a simple modality of the 'transcendental apperception.'

'Before the face of the other,' I have said. Can one, properly speaking, use the preposition *before* [*devant*] here? Have we not, in speaking thus, confused the meaning of the face with the plastic forms of representation that already mask it, whereas the face, in its formal nakedness, or stripped of forms, expresses mortality and signifies a commandment? Have we not already failed to recognize the incessant surplus of meaning that undoes these plastic forms? A surplus that cannot be represented – cannot be presented – but that signifies in the imperative with authority or glory. I must return, even if in a very general and rapid way, to the *how* of that glorious signifying of the commandment, to the 'imperativity,' so to speak, of that original imperative, that original transcendence.

The face of the other concerns me without the responsibility-for-the-other that it orders allowing me to go back to the thematic presence of a being that is the cause or source of this commandment. Indeed, it is not a question of receiving an order by first perceiving it and then obeying it in a decision, an act of the will. The subjection to obedience precedes, in this proximity to the face, the hearing of the order. Obedience preceding the hearing of the order – which gauges or attests to an extreme urgency of the commandment, in which the exigencies of deduction that could be raised by an 'I think' taking cognizance of an order are forever adjourned. An urgency by which the imperative is, 'dropping all other business,' categorical, and an irreversible subjection, i.e., that does not lend itself to the reversal of passivity into activity, to the reversal that characterizes intellectual receptivity, which always transforms itself into spontaneities of reception.

But 'subjection to an obedience preceding the hearing of the order' – is this just insanity and an absurd anachronism? Is it not rather the description of the paradoxical modality of inspiration, breaking precisely with the intellectualism of knowledge and tracing out, in obedience to the absolute order, the diachrony of the future itself? Is it not the unparalleled way in which, absolutely irreversible, the future commands the present without that way of concerning, without that 'affection' by the commandment and that passivity or patience, being reduced to any sort of 'simultaneity,' to any sort of superposition, be it partial or punctual, of the 'present' and the future – without the future's being dominated in the to-come [*à-venir*] or the *seizing* of an anticipation (or of a protention) – without the representation of fear or hope offending the dia-chrony of time and the excessiveness and the authority of the imperative? Inspiration breaks, precisely, with the intellectualism of knowledge: as if the order were formulated in the voice of the very one who obeys it. Such would be, beyond all metaphor, the voice of the ethical conscience, which is not the simple innateness of an instinct, or the intentionality in which the *I think* would continue to have the last word, investing that which imposes itself to it, transforming impatiently, in the 'realization,' its irreversible passivity into initiative, equaling what it welcomes, distorting all authority. The conversion of the for-itself into a for-the-other of responsibility cannot once again be played out in an autonomous for-itself, be it in the guise of a simple discovery made by the inflexible (but still reflecting on itself) 'I think' of a secret modality, hitherto unsuspected, of some 'profound nature.' The transcendence of inspiration.

The heteronomy of ethical obedience, which, in the guise of inspiration, is not the unfolding of a *vis a tergo*: it comes from *in front* [*de face*]: submission to the order issued [*signifié*] in the face of the other man which is not approached as a theme. Obedience to the absolute order – to the order par excellence – originary obedience to the order par excellence, to the word of God, on the condition of not naming God except on the basis of this obedience. An un-known God who does not take on a body, and who exposes himself to the denials of atheism!

But the meaning or content of that order is inseparable from the obedience subjected to its inspired order. What is ordered is responsibility for the other man, goodness wresting the *I* from its irresistible return to self, the wresting of the *I* from unconditional perseverance of a being in its being. One must underscore the unity between the *ethics* of this subjection to a commandment ordering responsibility for

35

the other and the *diachrony* of the future in that irreversible subjection that does not become inverted into knowledge and that, as if inspired, signifies *beyond* that which, in obedience, can be represented and presented. A *beyond* that the very 'imperativity' of the commandment and its goodness would signify to obedience. The concretization of the paradox of the idea of the infinite in Descartes' third *Metaphysical Meditation*, the *revelation* of transcendence behind all *unveiling* of truths.

Ethical inspiration and future – significance of prophecy. I would like to suggest the diachrony of the future, setting out from the prophetic inspiration that the impatience of anticipation in the Husserlian idea of aim, of intentionality and pro-tention does not equal. The idea of the Infinite taught by Descartes in his paradox, an unparalleled thought, thinking more than it can contain, the concrete wisdom of which I have tried to articulate in obedience to the commandment that, in the face of the other, dedicates me to the other man – that is a 'future aim' beyond what is to come [*l'à-venir*], the true 'phenomenology.' A thought thinking more than it thinks or a thought that, in thinking, does better than think, since it finds itself to be already responsibility for the other, whose mortality – and consequently whose life – regards me. A thought constrained to the categorical imperative, inspired by an unknown God, constrained to bear non-transferable responsibilities, but, thus, consecrating my personal uniqueness, my primogeniture and election. Dis-interestedness of a responsibility for the other and for his *past* – a past that for me is immemorial – on the basis of the *future* of prophesy – without which the un-known God would remain inaudible in his glory, breaking his negative theology without words – that is the temporality in which the intrigue of being and ontology is resolved in ethics.

2

Totality and Totalization

We recognize a whole when a multiplicity of objects – or, in a homogeneous continuum, a multiplicity of points or elements – form a unity, or come, without remainder, under a sole act of thought. Totality, that which makes a whole a whole, is also used as a synonym for the whole.

The ideas of whole and totality are implied in all thought and all experience. Like the categories, they form the latter, and as such, defy definition. All we can do is situate them in relation to other fundamental ideas, particularly to that of the part. In Kant's table of categories, totality is found among those of quantity, and as the synthesis of unity and plurality; in Aristotle, totality does not even appear where the enumeration of categories goes up to ten, but it is treated among the fundamental terms of thought in Book Delta of the *Metaphysics*.

'Totalization' may be understood to mean either the grouping of objects or of points in a whole, or the intellectual operation by which that multiplicity of objects or points is encompassed. The two meanings correspond to the extent that totalization and totality remain within the limits of sensible intuition, in which the totalizing thought is able to peruse all the elements of that intuition. We must begin by examining totality more closely at this level and see, in particular, how in examining how the thought that comes into play goes beyond intuition, while remaining on its scale or within its measure.

But thought conceives of totalities beyond totalities accessible to intuition, up to the whole that encompasses all things. The intellectual act rises from perception, in which everything is shown within the limits of the 'visible,' i.e. already as a part, to thought properly so called. This latter is not only an enlarged vision, and one that is enriched with memories, but also one that is panoramic and limited and conditioned by an encompassing whole. It intends henceforth the whole, understood to the very end and leaving nothing outside. But does the intellectual act not rise up in the void in this way? Do not such totalizations and totalities limit themselves to the pure form of the thinkable – to an absolutely indeterminate *something*, more devoid of content than the most general genera? Do they not belong to pure logic, moving between an *analysis* that distinguishes, in any whole, parts that it conditions, parts further divisible, either infinitely so, or down to the level of elements arbitrarily posited as absolutely simple, and a *synthesis* taking each whole as a part of a vaster whole that conditions it, thus going either to infinity, or, arbitrarily, to an absolute whole? Is totality, thought of in terms implied by such a formalization, still within the province of the true and the untrue? This is a Kantian problem: Does not the idea of absolute totality reduce to a pure concatenation of notions without any hold on reality? That would mean the divorce between the logical possibilities of thought for which rationality remains the basis, on one hand, and its [thought's] pretensions to knowledge of being, on the other.

The idea of totality can, however, be thought of outside the schema of intuition. Thinking totality would not consist in completing representation by making the rounds of the elements to be totalized. Far from reducing to a void, the totality of being would be the essence of Being itself, any given image offering only an abstract and partial aspect of the real. Truth is only truth when it is the whole of being. In this discordance between the whole and the given we can see, according to Hegel, reality in its rationality as a march toward the concrete universal, i.e. toward an entirely determined universal. The whole would presuppose a certain affinity of the parts among themselves, an organization. It would be a cosmos, a system, history. It would leave nothing else outside itself. It would be freedom.

This questioning of the formalism of totality is also reflected in the role played by the idea of totality in the exegesis of texts, in which the part to be understood owes its meaning to the whole from which it was taken, even though the whole cannot be understood without showing itself in its parts. Analysis and synthesis, far from being independent operations, presuppose one another reciprocally at every moment. The role played by totality in hermeneutics would then indicate that reason and totality are indeed inseparable, but that totality requires more than a spirit of continuity from reason.

The identification of the whole with the rational and being is not, however, the sole thought of the West. Issued from the Hellenic-Judeo-Christian tradition, it has had the anxiety of transcendence. To it, freedom in the guise of totality has also revealed a negative face of freedom. One must, consequently, ask whether it is human finitude alone that puts in question the totality whose antinomies Kant perceived, and whether the crisis of that idea does not come from the resistance that being puts up against it, or better yet, from the difference between being in its totality and the message of rationality.

I
THE WHOLE IN INTUITION

It is most remarkable that, in perception, the perceived groups itself immediately into multiple, separate things, sufficient unto themselves, so to speak – into totalities, independent from one another, the irreducibility of which the Gestalt psychologists, in particular, have underscored. Each one of these intuitive 'wholes' belongs to a vaster whole that conceptual thought isolates. But in the network of relations that science substitutes for perception, the concrete totalities of things are not just another step in a logical process. From Aristotle to Husserl, their meaning has been sought. The *whole* is 'that which contains the things contained in such a manner that they form a unit,' says Aristotle, and the unit is a characteristic property of natural things, so that the whole par excellence is conferred on natural things. They are whole by nature (*physei*), more eminently whole than are artificial objects. Man is more whole than any statue, a statue more whole than a number. A distinction is drawn between the sum (*pan*), in which the position of the parts is indifferent (water, all liquids, numbers) and the whole (*holon*), in which the position of the parts is not indifferent (the face, the hand) – the whole being applied to water or number by extension, by metaphor. The formal notion of totality is thus linked to a content. Can it legitimately be detached? The question will be asked from Kant to Hegel.

In Husserl, the whole is linked to the idea of concretization or 'independent content.' The dependent contents, being abstract (color and extension, sound and intensity, for example), are summoned to, and cannot exist outside of, the independence of the concrete. Concretization characterizes the whole. The whole is not contingent, as in Aristotle, upon the finality of the natural being. It does, however, require a content. But it is not reducible, in Husserl, to the fixity of the image that represents it. The kernel of the thing, circumscribed in its contours, given to perception in 'flesh and bones,' indicates the possibility of 'new determinations of that thing itself': a 'horizon.' The concrete whole is the datum along with its horizon. The totality thus remains open. It is the integration of aspects that confirm one another. When they infirm one another, the totality does not explode; each breaking open immediately reconstitutes, in another direction, the process of the totalization of aspects.

Despite its incompleteness, this intuitive whole is distinguished from the totality that encompasses things until the absolute totality of the world and that declares itself in the 'external horizon,' distinct from the interior horizon. The world is a totality on another model than the whole of the single object.

II
TOTALITY WITHOUT REALITY

The movement toward the ultimate totality, an absolute world or being, admits of differences, even in its formalism. The totality of individuals belonging to the same genus differs from the totality of men belonging to a nation, which in turn is different from the totality of episodes making up a story, from that of the points making up a space, or that of the members that make up an organism, or of words making up a language. Kant builds the idea of totality by setting out from the relation of conditioning, which is inscribed in the categories of the relation set forth in the 'Transcendental Logic,' and in which are contained all intuitive data *qua* data, insofar as they present themselves in experience to scientific understanding. Science seeks the condition of the datum, but only finds conditioned conditions. These suffice for the understanding of facts and the establishment of laws. They do not satisfy reason, which requires the regressive synthesis of the whole series of conditions back to the unconditional. Reason is that very requirement. It prescribes to understanding that it embrace all the actions of the understanding 'in an absolute Whole,' in thinking the ideas of the world and of God. Diverse aims of totality despite the formalism of totalization, the ideas of the world and of God go beyond the sensible datum. Kant shows that, to the degree that they go beyond it, they remain ideas that express no being. From the moment they are given an ontological significance, they turn reason against itself (antinomies) or make it speak nonsense. In the ideas of totality, reason thus loses its cognitive value. Its pretension to know would be illusory. In agreement with the rationalist tradition of the West, the idea of totality here again coincides with the ideal of integral intelligibility. It remains a *necessary illusion* and exerts a regulative function in scientific knowledge. But a gap separates henceforth reason and truth. Kant puts the ontological meaning of reason in question. As a datum, being is a part, it is never all, whereas thought can only direct itself toward being in directing itself toward the datum. A reality corresponding to the totality is not unthinkable. It is not known.

Discovering a rationality at the level of the sensible and the finite, in contrast with the inordinate rationality of the Platonic Idea, rediscovering the Aristotelian intelligibility inherent in things (which is expressed in the Kantian doctrine of schematism, in which the concepts of the understanding are exposed in time), Kant's criticist philosophy seriously shakes the foundations of the idea of totality. Henceforth the partial can have a meaning without the reality of the Whole and appearance can cease being dependent upon logical rationality. Since the absolute does not lend itself to totalization, one may wonder whether intelligibility is reducible to comprehension, to being encompassed without remainder. But we must also wonder whether the notion of being must not be rethought according to the idea of totality.

III
TRUTH IS TOTALITY

Being can only be true if it is totality. The true must include even errors, which, if excluded, would be 'elsewhere,' and would reduce the totality to a part, i.e., to an abstraction. Contrary to the Kantian conception of knowledge, true knowledge is a breaking away from the immediacy of the datum, from the intuitive. The latter, always circumscribed in its 'views' (though they may be assembled as they are imagined to be by a positivistic philosophy that considers itself to be the result of the sciences), is exclusive, partial, and depends upon 'points of view.' The true or the absolute, in which one can see, as Plato would say, 'the sun in its abode' (and not just in its reflections), can only be thought, without resulting from a synthesis that runs through the elements of a given series. The thought that thinks being in its totality is not a look placed in front of being. Representation, in which being is given to a thought still separated from it, is only being still in the state of indetermination or still insufficiently thinking thought.

The true function of totalizing thought does not consist in looking at being, but in determining it by organizing it. Whence the idea of the temporal or historical dimension of totality; history being not just any element to totalize, but totalization itself. The errors are truth to the degree that, in a given historical period, they express the still partial reality, but in the process of going toward its completion. Their partial character itself calls for their rejection, their negation, which, in the concrete, is produced by the action of reasonable men, that is, guided by the universal, transforming nature into culture or isolating reason from the immediate of the datum. There is, here, progression toward the whole, the movement of history itself, or the dialectic movement of thought.

Both superannuated truth and its negation are

'determinant' for the 'new' truth that 'does not fall ready-made from heaven,' but results from that historical determination. Error is kept in its being gone beyond. It is not outside of truth, which is total when no negation is any longer possible, or when no new determination is necessary. Totalization is the history of humanity *qua* realization of rational universality in mores and institutions, in which thought (the subject) is no longer out of step with that which is thought (substance), in which nothing remains other for reason, i.e., in which being is freedom.

The dialectical thought of totality allows one to grasp at once the whole and its parts, seen in the light of the whole; the whole being, as in Aristotle, the finality of the parts itself. Total presence of being to itself, or self-consciousness, the whole as the end of history is not empty; it is the reality in its concretization and most complete determination. A lucid and free humanity, of which the nineteenth century believed itself to be the glorious dawn.

IV
THE HERMENEUTIC TOTALITY

The constitution of a totality by the addition of parts is only conceivable in a mechanistic version of the world, in which one admits, as did Descartes, the possibility in being and thought of simple natures, intelligible by themselves (a totality that Aristotle describes as not dependent upon the disposition of the parts). The understanding of a text, a cultural work, is accomplished otherwise. It is true that it goes from the parts to the whole, but the parts derive their meaning from the totality. There would appear to be a circle in totalizing and analyzing thought that one would be tempted to call vicious, as the analysis and the synthesis mutually presuppose one another.

But the mutual presupposition of the analysis and the synthesis can lead to the recognition of what Heidegger called the 'hermeneutic circle,' which one would be wrong in calling vicious, since the circular movement of the totalization is precisely irreducible to a linear movement, operating in a homogeneous environment. In this circular movement, the whole and the parts determine one another. There are, in the understanding of the totality, progressive jumps, the first consisting in knowing how to enter into the hermeneutic circle, in getting beyond the immediacy in which the parts are given, as yet not understood as being parts. A notion of totality and of intellect that would lead to the understanding of all experience, and perhaps all reasoning on things, according to the model of the interpretation of texts. A notion of totalization that is ever to be resumed anew, an open notion of totality! A breaking away from the habits of Cartesian understanding, moving from the simple to the complex, without consideration of the light that the totality sheds on the comprehension of the simple. A conception in which the totality is the end of the parts, as Aristotle would have it, but also a conception in which, in an incessant to-and-fro movement, totality validates the part, which would justify a religious or personalist conception of man at the heart of creation, of which he would be both part and end.

V
BEYOND TOTALITY

Kant's critique of the idea of totality destabilized, but did not put in question, the potential of rationality for which a totalized universe seems to have the mission, and that was already able to prompt the pre-Socratics to formulate their wisdom by declaring that *all* is this or that *all* is that: water, fire or earth.

In the course of the history of Western philosophy, the impossibility of totalization itself has manifested itself on a number of occasions: in the dualism of opposed forces and values in Anaximander; in the Good and the notion of a *beyond Being* in Plato and Plotinus; as for being itself, in its equivocation that only admits of the unity of analogy and in the transcendence of the prime mover; in the idea that sustains the philosophy of a transcendent God that does not 'form a totality' with the creature; in Fichte's *Sollen*, which is not a simple powerlessness to think being, but n surpassing of being, irretrievable by the surpassed being, and which, in the final analysis, saves the latter from illusion; in the Bergsonian *durée*, which is the opening that puts back in question, on the basis of the Future, all completed totality before being the affirmation of I know not what mobile essence of being; in the critique of Western totality by Franz Rosenzweig, for whom God, the world and man no longer form the unity of a total sum. Do man and man form a totality any more than do these?

This impossibility of totalization is not purely negative. It traces out a new relation, a diachronic time that no historiography transforms into a totalized, thematized simultaneity, and the concrete accomplishment of which would be the relation of man to man, human proximity, peace among men, such that no synthesis taking form above their heads or behind their backs could dominate; a relation that, in the forms in which it seems to occur, in the form of a State, still draws its meaning from human proximity. Humanity would not be, on this view, one domain among those of the real, but the modality in which rationality and its peace are articulated wholly otherwise than in the totality.

3

Infinity

Philosophy has borrowed the notion of *the infinite* – correlative to that of the finite – from reflection on the exercise of knowledge, on one hand; from religious experience or tradition, on the other. These two sources determine the variety of meanings that are attached to this notion, the problems it raises and the evolution it undergoes in the course of the history of philosophy. The term itself is a substantivized adjective. It designates the property of certain contents offered to thought to stretch out beyond all limits. It is used in the first instance in cases in which limit has its apparently original meaning. It is appropriate to magnitudes of extension: to space, stretching out of sight, beyond the place we inhabit or look at; to time [*le temps*], from which the time of day [*l'heure*] is always torn loose; to the number series, none of which is the greatest – *quanta* making up a series. But the term infinite is also appropriate to magnitudes of continuity – to extensive or intensive *quanta continua*, in which no part of the whole is the smallest possible. The content diminishes ad infinitum. But *quanta*, the cradle of the infinite, are not its only domain. The infinite can designate a superlative qualitative excellence, above human measure or limits, the divinity of attributes enveloping the infinite with duration in the immortality of the gods, despite a certain finitude attested to by their multiplicity, which becomes conflicts and combat. But the infinite can also be situated above multiple infinities: the infinite One of the neo-Platonists, above all multiplicity (which discovers the perspective of infinity in which the Platonic idea of the Good-beyond-Being was placed), the One God of the Hebrew Bible brought into European history by Christianity. The Bible, though it does not use the term infinite (which in the Medieval Kabbala became the absolute name of God: En-Sof = in-finite), states a power beyond all power, that no creature, nor any other divinity, limits, and whose ways no one can know. The perfection of an inaccessible ideal, that no thought, no act could ever attain (though one might well wonder how that which is beyond act and thought succeeds in making itself known as such to the act of thought). Descartes said: '[But] I conceive God as actually infinite in so high a degree that nothing can be added to the sovereign perfection which he possesses.'[1] Here the notion of the infinite is close to the idea of transcendence. But it also resides in the idea of power itself, in the *will* that power presupposes, in the spontaneity that is precisely a way of being, without being determined by the outside, i.e., without having any limits. The Cartesian God will be infinite in this way: a will that is not even commanded by Good or Evil, Truth or Falsehood,

54

because it institutes them. Man's free will can, in this sense, in Descartes, also be said to be infinite. The equivalence between free will and the infinite without transcendence inspired the thought of the infinite in Fichte, Schelling and Hegel. It is again the will – the will of the will – or the will to power, that, in Nietzsche, describes the surpassing of man, the over-man. For a philosophy that judges transcendence to be out of reach for the thinking but finite being, the infinite is considered a methodological idea, a regulatory principle of the science of the finite, and assuring its progress. An idea and nothing but an idea, without counterpart in being.

But transcendence is not the only way to free oneself from limits. A being that had no *other* would be, by that very fact, infinite. The God of Spinoza, 'absolutely infinite being,' self-caused, signifies that extrinsic non-limitation, since all that is is in God, and nothing without God can either be or be conceived of; this absolute is accessible to intellectual intuition, which, distinct from the imagination, is characterized precisely by the fact of uniting itself – instead of remaining other – to the infinite that it contemplates. It is also the status Hegel recognizes in Spirit: the history of humanity, in which the thought of men overcomes specific bodies of knowledge and unilateral, exclusive institutions – contradicted or limited by others – and thinks in keeping with the universal, in such a way as to negate contradictory propositions in preserving them dialectically in some way in a coherent discourse. This latter institutes itself as a totality, in which all Other is included in the Same. The infinite would thus be absolute thought determining itself of itself, in a State and institutions by which, efficacious, it becomes Reality and through which the individual human being is free or infinite; as he will be free, in Marx, in a classless society resolving all contradictions and in which, consequently, an infinite is actualized. But to see the infinite in the suppression of the *Other* or in reconciliation with him assumes that the Other is, for the Same, nothing but limit and menace. Who would dispute that it is so, for the most part, in a human society subjected, like all finite reality, to the formal principle according to which the *other* limits or cramps the *same*: the wars and violence of the world, of all ages, is sufficient proof of that. But the other man – the absolutely other – the Other [*Autrui*] – does not exhaust his presence by that repressive function. His presence can be meeting and friendship, and in this the human is in contrast with all other reality. The face-to-face is a relation in which the *I* frees itself from being limited to itself (which it thus discovers), from its reclusion within itself, from an existence in which the adventures are but an odyssey, i.e., a return to the island. The exodus from that limitation of the *I* to itself, which is revealed in a whole series of reflections of contemporary philosophy on the meeting with the Other – from Feuerbach and

the course of the history of the notion of the infinite. The Infinite has contrived, in that history, to mean at once the irrational hiddenness of matter and the divinity (dissimulation or appearance) of God; the historical evolution of men being, then, nothing but the unfolding of the divinity of God, or the event – which requires no less than the history of humanity – of thought thinking itself, i.e., the event of rationality itself.

II
THE HISTORICAL GIVENS

The bad infinite

Classical thought, faithful to the ideal of completeness and measure that inspired its art and religion, was suspicious of the infinite. The hallmark of clouded thought corresponding to an unrealized reality, and lacking form to present itself to a knowledge capable of containing or representing it, the infinite – the *apeiron* – was indeterminateness, disorder, badness. But the finite forms, clear and intelligible, constituted the cosmos. The infinite, a source of illusion, got mixed up in it and had to be driven out, like the poets from Plato's city. Aristotle distinguished between potential and act, and hence the infinite *in potentia* of growth and division – in the order of matter – and the infinite *in actu*, which would be a flagrant contradiction. That contradiction was only to be overcome in the history of philosophy by a break with the quantitative notion of the infinite that Descartes took the precaution of calling the indefinite, and the traces of which Hegel would find even in the infinite of the should-be – *Sollen* – which he will contribute to disqualifying as the *bad infinite*. At the end of the nineteenth century and the beginning of the twentieth, the mathematician M. B. [*sic*] Cantor, finding operations on the infinite as well defined as those hitherto applied to actual, finite ones, will speak of *actual infinity* in mathematics; but that notion retains a rigorously operational meaning, derived from a modification of axiomatics. For Aristotle, to be means to be *in actu*, to be accomplished and completed. The definition or determination of the real excludes only the possible; it does not transform it [the real] into an abstraction detached from the totality of reality. And yet, as far as being apt to receive determination, the infinity of matter is not a nothing in classical thought. Among the pre-Socratics, the notion of infinity did not have an exclusively negative and pejorative meaning, even at the level of the spatial and temporal quantum. For Anaximander (sixth century BCE), a principle called *Apeiron*, unborn and incorruptible, is the source of all things, enveloping and directing them all, irreducible to any material element. It is of inexhaustible fecundity, and produces an infinite number of worlds. The cosmologists of the sixth and fifth centuries BCE took up the notion again: infinite time was linked with a perpetual cyclicality. From Heraclitus and Empedocles to the last Stoics, the idea of a cosmic periodicity was affirmed, worlds succeeding worlds in an uninterrupted time. There was not, between these worlds, any continuity or progress. But among the atomists, the idea of periodic returns replaced that of an infinite flow of time always bringing new things.

Plato 'will commit a parricide,'[2] in affirming, in opposition to 'his father,' Parmenides, that non-being, in a certain sense, is. All things include the unlimited, matter, place, a greater or lesser degree of extension, division and quality (more or less hot, more or less cold), infinity and indeterminateness, which are not pure nothings. But above all, without speaking of the infinite apropos of the idea of the Good, and without forbidding the look – after the journey and the exercise that its exorbitant brilliance requires – to fix that idea, Plato situates it beyond Being, thus opening, in a different sense than the quantitative one, the dimension of the infinite in which the infinite One of the neo-Platonists will be placed. As for Aristotle, in admitting the eternity of the world and its movement, he allows something like an actual infinity in the cause of this eternal movement. The act, purified of all potential, or form, purified of all matter, the Prime Mover or the God of Aristotle, sufficient unto itself as thought of its thought, is infinite in this new sense. Although Artistotle does not use the term, Saint Thomas will identify the infinite of the God of the Bible with the separation of pure form, and Hegel will recognize the actual infinite of the Absolute in the thought of the thought. That is how simplistic it is to contrast the finitude of classical thought with the infinity of modern thought. But the 'truth' of this commonplace resides in this: Space being for Aristotle the limit of bodies, the Aristotelian cosmos is finite, limited by the heavens and the fixed stars. This is a view of the heavens that had a determinate influence on cosmology until the dawn of the modern period.

The divine infinite

During the Hellenistic period, through Gnostic speculation and Christian patristics, a contact is established between Eastern spirituality and philosophy: the notion of infinity is identified with the perfection and omnipotence of the Biblical God. The One of Plotinus (205–270) is – by excess, not by defect – beyond any sensible or intelligible world. It is infinite, without form, beyond knowledge and activity, 'lacking all lack.' In it is concentrated that which, in the definite forms that emanate from it, disperses discursively into the infinity of matter. Finite, definite beings not only close themselves off from the infinity of matter, but remain torn away from the Infinite of the One. Its fullness is not confusion, but a more complete determination in which the lack that is constituted by the separation brought about by definition is lacking. The new idea of the infinite signifies precisely its compatibility with determination, as later, in the Kabbala, the *En-Sof*, the infinite God, 'buried in the depths of his negativity,' i.e., refractory to attributes, manifests himself in the attributes called *sefirot*, without degrading himself in that emanation, since that delimitation is also understood as an event at the heart of his hiddenness.

In Descartes and the Cartesians, the idea of perfection, which envelops those of completion and actuality, is inseparable from the idea of the infinite. 'The substance that we understand as being by itself sovereignly perfect and in which we conceive of absolutely nothing that contains any defect, i.e., any limitation to perfection, is called God.'

It is not without some difficulty that divine perfection and infinity are united. Origen (185–254) continues to put those who deny the limits in God by a 'simple love of fine discourse' on guard. To know is to define. An infinite God would not be known. The divine power must be tempered by his wisdom and his justice. But already for Saint Augustine it would be bringing God down to the human level to forbid his encompassing the infinite. For Jean Damascène (who died in 749), 'the Divine is infinite and inconceivable,' and 'the only thing that can be conceived of God is his infinity and his inconceivability.' For Thomas Aquinas (1225–74), the infinite is attributed to God to the extent that matter and power do not limit his form. The notion of the infinite loses its quantitative meaning. The infinite in God is thought of as actual infinity. The absence of limits takes on the meaning of independence, of sovereign will. But there is only an analogy between the infinite being in God and the finite being in the creature. A created infinite is absurd to Saint Thomas. There is no infinite multiplicity in the content of a spatial segment; its points are only infinite *in potentia*. As in Aristotle, the world is finite in space. Even time can be interpreted, according to Plato's Timaeus, as being born with the formation of the world. Roger Bacon (1214–94) continues to question the temporal infinity of the world, which would transform it into absolute power, into God. But henceforth finitude is a sign of imperfection, measuring the distance between the creature and God, who is perfect and infinite. And Duns Scotus (1265–1308), a partisan of the univocity of being, suggests that the creature resembles the Creator more than the philosophers of the analogy of being thought: the creature resembles him in man, by the will that 'commands the understanding.' 'Nothing other than the will is the total cause of the will's willing.' But we must wait until the Renaissance for the finite world of the Graeco-Roman astronomical system, like the Plotinian cosmos, to become open to the infinite.

It is the human soul (conceived, according to the biblical tradition, as being in the image of God) that, in the creature, is the first to receive the attribute of infinity. The way grace penetrates the soul could still, perhaps, be conceived according to the way the active intellect entered 'through the door' in the Aristotelian soul. But Duns Scotus already identifies that entry with a capacity for the infinite in the nature of the soul. For Meister Eckhart (1260–1331), finite creatures outside God are gifted with true reality in the same sense as divine reality. The thought of the Renaissance will recognize an infinite desire in the soul, which is not a simple lack. For Descartes, the idea of God is innate to the soul, and I am more certain of God than of myself: the finite is known against the background of the infinite. The intellectual priority of the infinite is henceforth added to its ontological priority. The meaning of the infinite in the creature also loses its quantitative meaning. It concerns the free will that nothing, not even the understanding, can command. The infinite as spontaneity, i.e. as freedom, will dominate the Western conception of the infinite. In Leibniz, that infinity-spontaneity of representation and will reflecting the infinite of God according to a functional law, particular to each monad, reconciles in God's creature the finite and the infinite. Nicholas of Cusa (1401–64) establishes a connection between God's infinity and the world's finitude: God is at once *implicitly* one and infinite and *explicitly* multiple and finite. The world according to space and time is the unfolding of the fullness that is *complicit* and actual in God, and that is, moreover, unknowable in itself (like the *En-Sof* of the Kabbalists), because any predicate would limit its infinitude. For us, infinity is the only positive predicate of God. But the finitude and multiplicity of the creature cannot be just finitude and nothing more, and lack perfection. They unfold God's infinitude. Not only does the human spirit, 'the sublime image of God,' take 'part in the fecundity of the creative being' by its infinite aspiration to knowledge, but the universe itself explicates, in time and space, the infinite complexity of God. The world is a concrete infinite, although Nicholas of Cusa does not call it *infinitum*, like God, but *indeterminatum*, not eternal but of infinite duration.

Infinity is the adequate measure of all that is: it is the finite straight line that is in potentiality and the infinite straight line in act, actualizing that which was only potential in the finite straight line. Henceforth, it is by the infinite that the finite is known – a thesis that is affirmed in Campanella (1568–1639), Descartes, Malebranche, Pascal, Spinoza and Leibniz. The indetermination of the world is the imitation of God's absolute infinity. The unlimited character of space acquires the dignity of a perfection, in counter-distinction from the Aristotelian order of values. Thus, outside rigorously scientific motives, it was a religious thought that determined the infinitism of modern science. Giordano Bruno (1548–1600) said to the inquisitors of Venice: 'I teach the infinite universe, the effect of the infinite power of God.'

Kepler is still afraid of the idea of an infinite world, without center, and that would thus exclude order. But Descartes, Leibniz, Newton and the young Kant affirm the infinity of spatio-temporal nature, relating it to God's infinity and the excellence of creation. Descartes distinguishes God's infinity, on the subject of which we understand that it cannot have any limits, and the indefiniteness of space, in which we see no reason for it to have any limits; but that does not prevent him from seeing in the indefiniteness of space the expression of the divine infinity. In Leibniz, the monad is not only the human soul; it is also the archetype of all being. The infinite of the soul is already the infinite of the universe. The best of all possible worlds reflects God's infinity. 'I am so much in favour of actual infinity', writes Leibniz, 'that instead of admitting that nature abhors it, as is popularly said, I hold that she shows it off everywhere, the better to mark the perfection of her Author.' (Letter to Foucher, Gerhudt edition, VI). Leibniz extends that thought of the infinite to the small and the divisible. 'Thus, I believe that there is no part of matter that is not, I do not say divisible, but actually divided, and, consequently, the least parcel must be considered as a world full of an infinite number of different creatures.' The most finite creature is filled with the infinite *in its own way*. Similarly, the actual infinity of the universe in its extension and divisibility is reflected in the actual infinity of the particular being through the infinite fullness of 'little perceptions.' The finitude of the being distinct from God's actual infinity consists in the fact that these little perceptions are not knowledge but remain obscure, and that each being reflects the same infinity *in its own way*. God knows these infinite reflections of the Infinite in the monads. 'The infinity of the future is entirely present to the divine understanding,' Kant wrote during his pre-critical period. Chapter 7 of Part 2 of his *Theory of the Heavens*[3] is titled 'Of the Creation in the Entire Extension of its Infinity, in Space as well as in Time.' Time is the 'successive completion of creation.' 'It requires no less than eternity to animate the innumerable and endless worlds, the entire extension of space.' The Kant of after the *Critique of Pure Reason* attributes a significance for free or moral action to that infinity. The categorical imperative is only valid if the subject is autonomous, i.e., not constrained and free, i.e., not limited by the other, or infinite. Kant adds to this, in order for it to take on its full meaning, the postulates of an unlimited length of time and an infinite being, God, the guarantor of the concordance between virtue and happiness. Kant's practical philosophy opens the way to the speculative philosophy of post-Kantian idealism.

All is infinite

According to the young Spinoza, divine goodness implies the total transferal of the divine to the creature. God's infinity and that of the world constitute but one, in Spinozism, and are differentiated only as *natura naturans* and *natura naturata*. 'By god, I understand an absolutely infinite being, i.e., a substance consisting in an infinite number of attributes, each of which expresses an eternal and infinite essence.' God infinitely infinite – the infinity of infinite attributes prevents the attributes' limiting God's infinity. An actual infinity 'by the force of its definition' or by the 'infinite enjoyment of being' (*per infinitam essendi fruitionem*), an infinity the parts of which are also infinite, and that it would be absurd to suppose divisible and 'measurable and composed of finite parts,' distinct from the infinity of duration, ' which has no limits, not by the force of its essence, but by that of its cause.' Infinite spatiality expresses the infinite essence of the divine substance in an immediate way; the appearance of infinite time translates the eternal *consecution* in the divine essence. An infinite number of modes express the attributes. Nothing is outside God's Infinite, so that all singularity is but the element of a chain of modifications and does not exist *qua* arbitrary, finite and contingent. We see in Spinoza the way the modes – an appearance of finite – absolutely affirm the absolute Infinite. *God is the cause of the modes in the same way that he is the cause of Himself.* And, lastly, the revelation of the Infinite is rationality itself. The infinite *cause of himself* is known by himself, i.e., is intelligibility par excellence. It is less clear why the Infinite in Spinoza is degraded in appearance. An ambitious philosophy, pursuing to the end the identification of the rational with the infinite will progressively reduce the knowable – always, in whatever form, given and exterior (and to which the incompleteness of positive science, the bad infinite, would still participate) – to this very process of surpassing: knowledge would thus be only knowledge of knowledge, and consciousness only self-consciousness, thought only thought of thought, or Spirit. Nothing would any longer be other: nothing would limit the thought of thought. The thought of thought is the infinite. But the surpassing of the *given* knowable – which Hegel calls *negativity* – is a process of determination. Its result is the concept. Hegel showed, precisely, that negativity is a determination and that determination is not completed with the limit of the defined and with exclusion: that it is totalization absorbing the *other*, or, concretely, the efficacious action of Reason in history. The singularity of consciousness itself is but the labor of the infinite inserting itself into the datum. The totality is not a piling up nor an addition of beings: it can only be conceived of as absolute thought that, without any other thing being an obstacle to it, affirms itself as absolute freedom, i.e., act, efficacious thought *qua* thought, actual infinity. The Classical ideal of knowledge as determination – or finitude – of intelligible forms and the rationality of surpassing thus meet. In Hegel's *Logic*, contrary to the conception of the Classical thinkers, the finite is not determinable in itself, but only in its passage to the other. 'The finite is something that is posited with its immanent frontier as the contradiction of itself by which it refers, and is forced, outside itself.' It is the very mode according to which the infinite is revealed. But it is the fact of revealing

itself, knowledge, that is the event of the Absolute
itself.

The finite without infinity

Kant's critique, in its rigorous distinction between
intuition, the pure form of which is time and in
which nature is *given*, and reason, which possesses the
idea of the infinite but cannot get a firm grip on
being, sets up the finite and the infinite in a new way.
As opposed to the Cartesian tradition, the finite, in
Kant, is no longer understood in light of the infinite.
Integrating the teachings of empiricism, Kant relates
the *appearing* of Nature to human sensibility, which
is the condition of a finite being, whose only way of
relating to the Real is by being affected, impressed,
receptive. Appearing nature thus bears the mark of
the subject's finitude. That mark consists not only in
the subjective character of sensation – at once state of
soul and quality of object – but, more profoundly, in
the rigorously successive character of the regressive
synthesis carried out by science, which apprehends
and comprehends the real. The successive is marked
by the subject because the regressive scientific synthesis, which takes the datum back to its preconditions,
cannot transcend its incompleteness. It does not suffice for the subject to reason thus: 'If the conditioned
is given, the unconditioned condition *or* the totality
of conditions is given,' precisely because the so-called
totality is here but temporal succession and not the

eternity of a logical consecution; because time is time
and not an actual infinity. The finite – temporal –
way of apprehending the real thus belongs to the
objectivity or reality of the real. The infinite, a
regulative idea, does not *constitute* the datum. The
infinity of the idea is only actualized at the price of
an illusion called transcendental appearance, Reason
illicitly leaping over time. The motives that guide
reason toward the infinite do not depend on the
function of the understanding, which assures, according to the schema of time, the synthesis necessary for
the unification of the sensible and the apprehension
of the datum. What does it matter if the principles of
understanding, like those of reason, derive, for Kant,
from formal logic! The indefiniteness of the temporal
series is not the obscure or the confused, of which the
infinity of the idea would be the clear and distinct.
The finite is not related to the infinite. Kant's transcendental dialectic confirms the Kantian doctrine on
the schematism of the concepts constitutive of Nature,
expounding, against the incipient Hegelian era, the
irreducibility of the datum as such – of the finite – to
the movement of systematization and totalization and
dialectic transcendence. One must point out the
agreement of these positions with the meaning the
infinite takes on in science, which is at once open to
an infinite universe and – prudence more than wisdom – conscious of its essential incompleteness. In
Husserlian phenomenology, we find the Kantian way
of describing the finite independently of the infinite,

and the thesis that each form of objectivity has its own finite modes of apprehension, which mark the very objectivity of the objects. The idea in the Kantian sense of the term, i.e., the Kantian infinite as a regulative idea, not realizable in being – a non-actual infinite – guides, in that phenomenology, which is mainly idealist in this, the constitution of the object on the basis of the finite datum: it illuminates the infinite horizon on which the datum appears, and the infinite horizon of horizons. Finally, in Heidegger, the finitude of being is not the equivalent of a negation of the infinite. On the contrary, it is on the basis of positive structures of existence – being-in-the-world, care and being-toward-death – that finitude is described. It is by setting out from finite temporality and through the leveling and banalization of that finite temporality that Heidegger deduces infinite time. And on the last page of his *Kant and the Problem of Metaphysics*, Heidegger teaches that 'nothing is as radically repugnant to ontology as the idea of an infinite being.' While leaving open the question of whether finitude does not 'presuppose' some infinitude, Heidegger is far from thinking that that 'presupposition' brings us purely and simply back to the Cartesian positions and themes, since he asks, always writing the word 'presupposition' in quotation marks: What is the nature of this 'presupposition'? What does infinitude, posited in this way, mean? Bergson, like Heidegger, and prior to him, teaches a time that is irreducible to an infinite series of instants treated as an eternity by the intelligence. The time composed of homogeneous instants, a superficial, degraded time, turns us toward *durée*, the instants of which in a sense transcend themselves, laden with all their past and already charged with a future; in the very limit of the past, surging forth new; old with the age of being, and as if at the first day of creation, creative, freeing themselves of their limitations, infinite. The true dimension of the past would be the interiority that is *durée*. An infinity of the possible, more precious than the actual infinity. But is not the bad infinity at the bottom of all the triumphant infinities? That is perhaps the thought of Maurice Blanchot, who, in the depths of being, hears the monotonous sound of a ceaseless rainfall, devoid of meaning. We should also note the new sense that Heidegger conferred on the finite and the infinite. They are no longer the attributes of beings [*étants*], to which they would be related in Western metaphysics, which, according to Heidegger, consists in understanding being [*être*] on the basis of the beings that being manifests. It is the being of beings that would be referred to by the terms finite and infinite, thus responding to the ontological problem, to the understanding of being that determines, in Heidegger's view, the history of philosophy and of history *tout court*. Hence new light is shed on many of the great texts on infinity, and even certain ways of speaking, such as the gerund in Spinoza's *infinita essendi fruitio*.

III
INFINITY AND ETHICS

In the context of knowledge in which it appeared to Western thought, the Infinite absorbs the finite, presents itself as the Same overcoming the Other, a thought of thought, becoming *omnitudo realitatis*. But in that divinization of the Infinite, have we not lost the specifically religious divinity of the God who permitted the idea of infinity to dominate Western rationalism? For a theology that made gnosis into the very object of its gnosis, all relation to the Infinite that was not knowledge would be taken for a representation without a concept, for the childhood of absolute thought. One may, however, wonder whether a different path is not possible. The presence, taught by Descartes, of the Idea of the infinite in a soul created too small to contain it, indicates that its alterity neither limits nor absorbs, [but] that it elates the soul that, according to formal logic, it should harm. That the alterity of the Infinite can consist in not being reduced, but in becoming proximity and responsibility, that proximity is not a failed coincidence but an incessant – and infinite – and, so to speak, glorious growth of alterity in its call to responsibilities, which, paradoxically, increase as they are taken; that the finite is, thus, as if for the greater glory of the Infinite – that is the formal design of the notion of infinity that, when taken as knowledge, is lowered. 'I have never treated the infinite except to submit to

75

it,' Descartes wrote to Mersenne on 28 January 1641, showing in the very knowledge of the Infinite already a beyond knowledge. The proximity of the other showing me his or her face, in society with me, and the implications of that encounter overturn the logical and ontological play of the same and the other, transforming it into ethics. An entire strain of contemporary philosophy, setting out from the irreducibility of the interpersonal to relations of objectivity, thematization and knowledge, is situated in the religious tradition of the idea of the infinite. One may wonder whether it is not drawing close to that tradition, even when it expresses itself in a deliberately and rigorously atheistic way.

II

PHILOSOPHY OF DIALOGUE
AND FIRST PHILOSOPHY

4

Beyond Dialogue

The ten points of Seelisberg – approved in July, 1947 by an international conference against anti-Semitism – the twentieth anniversary of which we are celebrating today, is addressed to Christians. They formulate resolutions on the way they should, in future, speak of the Jews and teach about Judaism. This text does not tell Jews what they should think about Christians. Doubtless on this point our long cohabitation in Europe, our co-citizenship in the modern nations, our communion on the benches of lay schools, studying Bossuet, Racine and Pascal, have not led to any form of underestimation or disdain. Doubtless also, the fact of Hitlerism's having been possible in a Europe that had been evangelized for fifteen centuries has not closed the eyes of Jews to the charity and abnegation shown by Christians during a period in which, among brown shirts, the black robe promised support, comfort or at least understanding.

The Seelisberg text deals mainly with the catechism, attempting to rectify its perspective. It is obvious that Judaism, unless it recants, can recognize itself neither when it is condemned in theological terms, nor when in theological terms it is rehabilitated. But the ten points of Seelisberg – this new Decalogue – attests to a concern to remind Christians of the perpetuity and universality of the Old Testament and the dignity of those who, according to a Talmudic apology, ravished from the angels their secret, in committing themselves to accomplish the commandments before hearing the dogmas upon which they are based. To adhere to an ethics without worrying about its doctrinal presuppositions, to set one's metaphysics according to categorical imperatives – is surely to proceed in the way most in keeping with the Biblical spirit.

The Seelisberg principles, too, have found an elite capable of that angelic 'inversion' in which the ethical precedes doctrine, and does not worry about the dogmatic upsets it presages. In twenty years one does not rectify the bad habits and mistakes of twenty centuries. But groups called Judeo-Christian Friendships formed everywhere. The French one is also celebrating its twentieth anniversary. It must be associated with the homage that is due to the principles and men of Seelisberg. The fact is, the Seelisberg conference was already the work of Judeo-Christian associations of various countries; thus it expressed the good will of our Christian friends who did not even wait for these ten points to become our friends. It is therefore an unconditional friendship, impatient to act and to preach by example, that we celebrate tonight.

The struggle against anti-Semitism – at Seelisberg, in the Judeo-Christian Association – concerns primarily the conscience of non-Jews. But we are too closely allied to the spiritual life of our contemporaries not to participate in their case of conscience. Besides, how can we remain indifferent when a détente in human relations is attested or announced? How can we not take the hand extended with such confidence, sincerity and warmth? That is why, shortly after the war, there was not only judeophilia, but Judeo-Christian friendships. That is why there were Jews at Seelisberg. Their position has not always been ... comfortable. Believe us, it is not always agreeable – or it is not unreservedly so – to receive excuses, praise and declarations attributing to you an advantageous role in the metaphysical drama. Even in the Amitié judéo-chrétienne [Judeo-Christian Amity], that advantageous position has not always been comfortable. From the outside, it appears suspect of ambiguity: for some, the Jews adopt an air of permanent gravity, the better to accuse and vindicate; for others, they appear to expose themselves to abandoning their faith by dint of being pitied. Despite all these years of progressive forgetting, no one among us can cure the stigmata of so many burns, nor pardon nor absolve in the place of those who have died. But to practice Judeo-Christian friendship does not consist in enjoying the role of victim, nor in allowing oneself to be seduced by compassion.

Thinking now of the Jewish promoters of this new movement of good will, Edmond Fleg and Jules Isaac, and the great masters who have disappeared (to

81

which we must also add the name of the great
militant, Maurice Vanikoff), I would like to distinguish the different meanings that Judeo-Christian
friendship can take on for us, and to say, in con-
clusion, the meaning it assumes for those who are
here twenty years afterward, when after all so many
things have changed. There no longer is any Jewish
Magisterium, as you know. Israel is a community of
persons studying the same books. Each person speaks
for himself or herself. But each in his sincerity bears witness to an aspect of the truth, and it is these various
aspects that I would like to mention briefly. Edmond
Fleg and Jules Isaac, assimilated Western Jews,
rejoined the community of Israel after the two crises
that struck European Jewry, the Dreyfus Affair and
Hitlerism. Edmond Fleg was overcome by the Dreyfus Affair. The triumph of truth did not make him
forget the bitterness of the struggle that had led to it.
He did not believe the rehabilitation of Dreyfus
suppressed the last contradiction of our society. But
the painful life of Edmond Fleg revealed an almost
inexhaustible power of hope. Judeo-Christian friendship certainly represented for him an attachment to
the common values that his work does not cease to
exalt. The point at which the paths separate is indicated very precisely in *Jésus raconté par le Juif errant*
[Jesus told by the Wandering Jew][1]. That point is
situated much further than that of the parting of
ways. But for Fleg, after the separation itself, the
Jewish soul retains enough love to remain fraternal.

The attitude of a Fleg translates an experience of kinship with Christianity. We recognize ourselves in this relationship whenever we are in the presence of a world that does not know, or does not want to know, the Bible, like that Pharoah at the beginning of Exodus – 'a new sovereign who did not know Joseph.' Who will deny that the presence of that world at the threshold of our own is not the characteristic trait of the period we are entering? I am not thinking exclusively of our kinship in the face of Nazism. But behold, upon the world's stage, innumerable masses advancing out of Asia. In the eyes of these crowds who do not take sacred history as their frame of reference, are we Jews and Christians anything but sects quarreling over the meaning of a few obscure texts? Through the two billion eyes that watch us, History itself stares us down, shredding our subjective certainties, uniting us in one common destiny, inviting us to show ourselves able to measure up to that human wave, inviting us to bring it something other than distinctions and anathema.

With uncompromising intransigence before the truth, and in opposition to the teaching of disdain, of which he directly accused historical Christianity, but also with uncompromising intransigence before the truth, of which he proclaimed, as a humanist and scholar, the virtue of reconciliation, Jules Isaac struggled *for* and *in* Judeo-Christian friendship. Without that element, Jews could only receive friendship as commiseration or as a pardon, granted after a long quarrel to a survivor who has done many wrongs, but also suffered much hardship. It is true that Judaism cannot lay claim to more innocence than the rest of humanity. And because of the supplementary obligations that it feels, and imprudently calls 'election,' it is an unhappy consciousness, unhappier than other unhappy consciousnesses. But Jules Isaac has made possible an essential refusal. He rejected the guilt imposed upon the Jews solely for a certain theology. A guilt that separated them from all human warmth. Many of us do not even consent to Jules Isaac's language, in which too much theology is still intertwined with history. But for all of us the essential element of his thesis stands: rejection of the Mephistophelian guilt of one who does good in willing evil, or who assured the salvation of the world because he alone had the soul of an executioner.

But the years that have gone by may not have accomplished all that seemed possible to a Fleg or a Jules Isaac immediately after the Liberation. The acuity of the apocalyptic experience lived between 1933 and 1945 is dulled in memory. The extraordinary returns to order. There have been too many novels, too much suffering transformed on paper, too many sociological explanations and too many new worries. I would now like to say what, from my perspective, despite the changed situation, I have found to be unique in the Judeo-Christian Amity of Paris – during the little meetings held from time to time under the presidency of Jacques Madaule. I came late to this circle, and with a certain degree of hesitation. Not for religious reasons. I feared that adherence to an association created with a view to bringing Jews and Christians closer together might express ingratitude toward the lay spirit, which, by other means, has united so many human groups separated by a variety of beliefs and philosophies into one republic.

The spirit I found there immediately appeared to me not as a return to superannuated forms, anterior to the constitution of an egalitarian and homogenous society, but as presupposing that homogeneity and going even further, and even more deeply, in the spirit of equality and fraternity.

We are used to thinking of history as a harmonious process in which all problems are resolved, all conflicts settled, in which, in universality, all contradictions are reconciled. We approach already accomplished history. Already Saint-Exupéry's boa (whom one of my students once alluded to in this connection) has swallowed the elephant without chewing. And it is already digesting it.

What a watchful attention to history in the making reveals – besides the many problems awaiting their resolution from reason, technology or dialogue – is the existence of insoluble problems; problems inherently insoluble, and delivered over to violence, not just because of our passions, our impatience and our laziness, but because of the dormant antinomy within them. Smothered by violence, they return, after the blood and the tears, in the form of other insoluble problems.

Perhaps the Judeo-Christian problem, when thought through to the end, is one of those insoluble problems, because Judaism and Christianity are part of the same drama, and not different enough not to challenge one another. And surely the Judeo-Christian problem is not the only insoluble one. And perhaps a Jewish existence is caught up in many insoluble problems; and perhaps in speaking of that this evening I am not, as one might think, deflecting the Jewish testimony that I must bear toward metaphysics. There are oppositions between men that, at first blush, seem, like so many others, to do no more than give rise to reflection and discussions, call for committees, conferences and institutions, to dispel violence. One soon perceives that all the difficulties they contain can, in fact, be overcome. All but one. And that last difficulty remains insoluble and annoying because, without realizing it and out of patience, the minds dealing with it turn toward violence and guile, speak of conversion and expulsion, of using force and driving into the sea – of too bad about this or that or the other thing. After violent thoughts, brought on by argumentative thoughts, pity is no more.

Judeo-Christian Amity, such as I have seen it practiced in this group (the only one I know), the Judeo-Christian Amity of Paris and its president have shown me, issuing from the specific cause that lights its way, a new attitude, a paradigm of the one that seems to me to be missing in the perfect deductions of the sublime doctrinaires of progress: the search for a proximity beyond the ideas exchanged, a proximity that lasts even after dialogue has become impossible. Beyond dialogue, a new maturity and earnestness, a new gravity and a new patience, and, if I may express it so, *maturity and patience for insoluble problems*. Those who, under the presidency of Mr Madaule, practice Judeo-Christian Amity in Paris, have renounced proselytism and propaganda, not in order to find some most-common-denominator platform, but because they have understood that in certain conflicts persuasion itself is violence and repression.

Neither violence, nor guile, nor simple diplomacy, nor simple tact, nor pure tolerance, nor even simple sympathy, nor even simple friendship – that attitude before insoluble problems, what can it be, and what can it contribute?

What can it be? The presence of persons before a problem. Attention and vigilance: not to sleep until the end of time, perhaps. The presence of persons who, for once, do not fade away into words, get lost in technical questions, freeze up into institutions or structures. The presence of persons in the full force of their irreplaceable identity, in the full force of their inevitable responsibility. To recognize and name those insoluble substances and keep them from exploding in violence, guile or politics, to keep watch where conflicts tend to break out, a new religiosity and

solidarity – is loving one's neighbour anything other
than this? Not the facile, spontaneous *élan*, but the
difficult working on oneself: to go toward the Other
where he is truly other, in the radical contradiction
of their alterity, that place from which, for an insufficiently mature soul, hatred flows naturally or is
deduced with infallible logic. One must deliberately
abstain from the convenience of 'historical rights,'
'rights of enrootedness,' 'undeniable principles' and
'the inalienable human condition.' One must refuse
to be caught up in the tangle of abstractions, whose
principles are often evident, but whose dialectic, be it
ever so rigorous, is murderous and criminal. The
presence of persons, proximity between persons: what
will come of this new spirituality, that proximity
without definite projects, that sort of vigilance without dialogue that, devoid of all definition, all thought,
may resemble sleep? To tell the truth, I don't know.
But before smiling at *maturity for insoluble problems*,
a pathetic formula, actually, let us think, like one of
my young students, of Saint-Exupéry's little prince,
who asks the pilot stranded in the desert, who only
knows how to draw a boa constrictor digesting the
elephant, to draw a sheep. And I think what the little
prince wants is that proverbial lamb who is as gentle
as a lamb. But nothing could be more difficult. None
of the sheep he draws pleases the little prince. They
are either violent rams with big horns or too old. The
little prince disdains the gentleness that only comes
with extreme age. So the pilot draws a parallelogram,

the box in which the sheep is sleeping, to the little prince's great satisfaction.

I do not know how to draw the solution to insoluble problems. It is still sleeping in the bottom of a box; but a box over which persons who have drawn close to each other keep watch. I have no idea other than the idea of the idea that one should have. The abstract drawing of a parallelogram – cradle of our hopes. I have the idea of a possibility in which the impossible may be sleeping.

5

The Word I, the Word You, the Word God

Despite all that may have been said against science, we must not forget that, amid the deterioration of so many human orders, scientific research remains one of the rare domains in which man controls himself, bows to reason, is not wordy or violent, but pure. These are moments of research, constantly interrupted by the banalities of everyday life, but moments that, conjoined, have their own duration. Is not the place of morality and loftiness henceforth the laboratory? Is it not there that the soul is alone with being, in an intimacy no desert hermitage could equal? The object under investigation permits not the least dishonesty, and is unforgiving.

But the idealist critic of the notion of substance during the last century, the phobia of alienation and reification, and, closer to us, Bergsonism, phenomenology and the philosophy of existence have made us suspicious of the quasi-natural tendency to take the *object* as the model of reality, objectivity as the being of what is, and science as true contact with the world.

Other models of the Real are then praised and described: relation, durée, history, the person, the instrumentality of the means of production and of physical objects, and human 'finitude.' *There is a bringing out of the meaning that informs concrete life*: economic behavior, creative intuition, savoir-faire, feelings, immediate sensible perception; also, the contradictions between thinkers and the struggles among men, which announce the dialectic and its reconciliations. These constitute so many different ways of approaching the verb *to be*, which would be at the birth of all meaning. The term *modality* no longer designates just the *possible*, the *real*, and the *necessary* of formal logic, but a variety of different ontological structures.

The wisdom to which the new reflection aspires, and the life it expresses, consist nonetheless in encompassing the universe. While condemning the intellectualist asceticism of the laboratory, we are still persuaded that the signifying of meanings, or rationality, is still constructed the same way knowledge is: an intention that encompasses – includes – an externality.

The most spontaneous *lived experience* splits in two in order to become intimate in rejoining itself. It already reflects on itself in its naïve spontaneity. We hold to the image we have experienced, and make ourselves memories. Enjoyment and suffering are experience. To live in a meaningful way is *to know* life in living it. All that philosophy of *the concrete* continues, in a way, the classical tradition, in which intelligibility was only a relationship with the world, with being in its neutrality of the 'there is,' the articulated integration of the totality of the data without remainder, pursued to the possibility of saying a sovereign *I*.

The relation that Martin Buber, born exactly one hundred years ago, extracted from the word *you*, as opposed to the objectivity of the *that*, and which was to flower into 'dialogical philosophy,' seems at first to confirm this movement 'toward the concrete,' so named by Jean Wahl in an important work by that title in 1932. In it, Wahl speaks especially of Gabriel Marcel, who, in his *Metaphysical Journal*, published in 1927, without having read Buber, established the originality and importance of the relation between the *I* and the *you*.[1]

To say 'you' is the primary fact of Saying [*Dire*]. All saying is direct discourse or a part of direct discourse. Saying is that rectitude from me to you, that directness of the face-to-face, directness of the encounter par excellence, of which the geometer's straight line may be just an optic metaphor. Directness of the face-to-face, a 'between us' [*entre-nous*], already conversation [*entre-tien*], already dia-logue and hence *distance* and quite the opposite of the contact in which coincidence and identification occur. But this is precisely the distance of proximity, the marvel of the social relation. In that relation, the difference between the *I* and the other remains. But it is maintained as the denial, in proximity which is also difference, of its own negation, as non-in-difference toward one another. Like the non-indifference between close friends or relatives. Being concerned by the alterity of the other: fraternity. The source of the gratuitous hatred and disinterested devotion, but an affectivity distinct from the love that, like hunger, attaches itself to what can satisfy: an affectivity not to be confused with the one involving the passions of the soul, needs satisfied or unmet, nerve endings and visceral changes.

An extra-ordinary relation. From Buber's and Marcel's first description of it, the word God is pronounced, as if it shed light upon the space in which the rectitude of the dialogue can take form. You par excellence. 'Eternal' you, offering itself to invocation rather than observation or experience: an invisible God. The pronoun *you* is not put in place of some noun to designate a substance: a *this* or a *that* that would in addition be qualified as *you*. Here the nominative of the noun is left behind by the vocative, which is not the denomination of beings. The thesis with which Buber's *I and Thou* opens affirms that the I-You relation is not reducible to the I-It. The *you* does not presuppose the *that*. A logical paradox, a counter-natural figure, that way in which the *you* does not rest on a *that* in the neutrality of the 'there is' is the opening up of a dimension in which *to mean* does not refer to being. God is conceived of outside the world or beyond being, in dis-inter-estedness.

But such a topography, in Buber more clearly than in Marcel, only appears before the other *man* approached in the *you*. Here begins the itinerary of the beyond, without our needing – before the human face – in order to define the excessive term, transcendence, any words other than this pronoun, and without being able to find some language capable of reabsorbing the illusion that would be its origin. For that illusion would itself only be excessive, unless it should be the hyperbole of transcendence itself.

In our spiritual heritage, love of one's neighbour accompanies religious life. But it would at best be only the second commandment, after the love of God. And that ethics, according to the theologians, would never equal the true essence of the relation to God, always understood as being. At the religious level, morality would be considered something we have moved beyond. What seems to me to be suggested by the 'philosophy of dialogue' is that the encounter with the other man takes place neither on a side-street nor a detour, nor some parallel track of transcendence, and that the face of the other bears the trace of its straightest, shortest and most direct movement.

'*If there is a God, we must love Him only and not the creatures of a day*,' says Pascal.[2] It is according to being – to its permanent or passing nature – that love, on this view, would be measured. The fact that fraternity can mean the annulment, or the eclipse, of that ontological importance of attachment, that a different importance, a different 'above all else,' a different absolute can move us, that beyond the weight of the neighbour in being or in nothingness, without ontology, fraternity can take on an importance in excess, a fraternity through which the God who 'opens up my lips' (*Psalms* 51:17) immediately becomes meaningful – that is the great novelty of a way of thinking in which the word God ceases orienting life by expressing the unconditional foundation of the world and cosmology, and reveals, in the face of the other man, the secret of his semantics.

6

The Proximity of the Other

You wrote in Totality and Infinity: *'First philosophy is an ethics.' Do you mean that philosophy addresses itself to what is most urgent to us as human beings?*

When I speak of first philosophy, I am referring to a philosophy of dialogue that cannot not be an ethics. Even the philosophy that questions the meaning of being does so on the basis of the encounter with the other.

This would be a way of subordinating knowledge, objectification, to the encounter with the other that is presupposed in all language.

To address someone expresses the ethical disturbance produced in me, in the tranquility of the perseverance of my being, in my egotism as a necessary state, by the interruption of the 'conatus essendi' [effort to be] (an expression of the being of being in Spinoza).

A going outside oneself that is addressed to the other, the stranger. It is between strangers that the encounter takes place; otherwise, it would be kinship. All thought is subordinated to the ethical relation, to the infinitely other in the other person, and to the infinitely other for which I am nostalgic. Thinking the other person is a part of the irreducible concern for the other. Love is not consciousness. It is because there is a vigilance before the awakening that the *cogito* is possible, so that ethics is before ontology. Behind the arrival of the human there is already the vigilance for the other. The transcendental *I* in its nakedness comes from the awakening by and for the other.

All encounter begins with a benediction, contained in the word 'hello'; that 'hello' that all *cogito*, all reflection on oneself already presupposes and that would be a first transcendence. This greeting addressed to the other man is an invocation. I therefore insist on the primacy of the well-intentioned relation toward the other. Even when there may be ill will on the other's part, the attention, the receiving of the other, like his recognition, mark the priority of good in relation to evil.

Your thought would be an attempt to exit what you call the formless, the 'there is,' the phenomenon of impersonal being without generosity. How does being move from non-sense to 'something that is'?

This concept of the 'there is' represents the phenomenon of the absolutely impersonal. 'There is' posits the simple fact of being, without there being any objects. The being in every silence, every non-thought, every way of withdrawing from existence.

'There is' [*il y a*], in the same way as it is raining [*il pleut*], it's nice out [*il fait beau*]. This 'it' marks the impersonal nature of the stage in which impersonal consciousness saw that there is something, without object, without substance – a nothing that is not a nothing, for this nothing is full of murmuring, but of a murmuring that has not been named. In that horrifying experience of naughting, the thematics of the 'there is' grounds the construction of a subject that, from the neuter, will affirm itself, posit itself. From the 'there is,' the enveloping presence of anonymity, which weighs heavily on the human being, subjectivity emerges, despite that which annuls it. This first exiting from self, an eruption from being, begins with the recognition of things [*choses*], but it is also a stage of the enjoyment of life, of self-sufficiency. This love of self is an egotism that founds being and constitutes the first ontological experience. This experience foreshadows the opening and true exiting from self. The human will pass through another decisive step, in which the subject, despite its satisfaction, fails to be sufficient unto itself. All exiting from self represents the fissure that opens up in the same toward the other. Desire metamorphosed into an attitude of openness to exteriority. Openness that is appeal and response to the other. The proximity of the other, origin of all putting into question of self.

If Martin Buber conceived of an I-You relation, complete reciprocity, you would like that encounter to be

99

transcended in the relation of the subject to the Other, who would be much more than a you, apparently.

The other would be alterity itself, and an unattainable alterity.

Martin Buber was indeed the first to conceive of the distinction between a thing that is, and a thing that is 'that' for me, an object that I can know. He then contrasted to 'that' a relation to the other, who is not an object, who is not a thing, and who is the one to whom I say you. He consequently contrasted the I-You relation to the I-It one. He thought that the I-You relation is irreducible to the I-It, and that the social relation to the other presents a total autonomy with respect to the observation of things and with respect to knowledge. The social relation cannot be knowledge because the correlate to that social relation is a human being to whom I say you.

So I wondered whether the true relation to the other rests on that reciprocity that Buber finds in the I-You relation. Buber says that when I say you, I know that I am saying you to someone who is an *I*, and who says you to me. Consequently, in that I-You relation, we are immediately in society, but in a society in which we are equal in relation to one another. I am to the other what the other is to me.

My interrogation consisted in questioning that initial reciprocity. The other whom I address – is he not initially the one with whom I stand in the relationship one has with one who is weaker? For example, I am generous toward the other without that generosity being immediately claimed as reciprocal. Although Buber is one of the first thinkers to put the accent on an I-You relation in conjunction with an I-That, this concept of reciprocity bothered me, because the moment one is generous in hopes of reciprocity, that relation no longer involves generosity but the commercial relation, the exchange of good behavior. In the relation to the other, the other appears to me as one to whom I owe something, toward whom I have a responsibility. Hence the asymmetry of the I-You relation and the radical inequality between the I and the you, for all relation to the other is a relation to a being toward whom I have obligations. I insist, therefore, on the meaning of that gratuitousness of the 'for the other,' resting on the responsibility that is already there in a dormant state. The 'for the other' arises within the *I*, like a command heard by him, as if obedience were already being [*l'être*] listening for the dictate. Alterity's plot is born before knowledge. But that apparent simplicity of the relation between the I and the You, in its very asymmetry, is yet again disturbed by the arrival of the third person, who stands next to the other, the you. The third party is also a neighbour, a face, an unattainable alterity.

Here, with the third party, we have the proximity of a human plurality. Between the second and the third person, there can be relations in which one is guilty toward the other. I pass from the relation in which I am obligated to the other, responsible for the other, to one in which I ask myself which is first. I ask the question of justice: Which one, in that plurality, is the other par excellence? How can one judge? How to compare others – unique and incomparable? The person for whom one is responsible is unique, and the one who is responsible cannot delegate his or her responsibility. In this sense, the latter is also unique. In the time of knowledge and objectivity, beyond and on the hither side of the nakedness of the face, Greek wisdom begins.

I now pass from the relation without reciprocity to a relation in which there is reciprocity, equality, between the members of a society. My search for justice presupposes just such a new relation, in which all the excess of generosity that I must have toward the other is subordinated to a question of justice. In justice there is comparison, and the other has no privilege with respect to me. Between persons entering into that relation, a relationship must be established that presupposes comparison between them, i.e., presupposes a justice and a citizenship. A limitation of that initial responsibility, justice nonetheless marks a subordination of me to the other. With the arrival of the third party, the problem of fundamental justice is posed, the problem of the right, which initially is always that of the other. Jankélévitch worded it well: 'We don't have any right; it is always the other who has rights.' It was indispensable to know what number two is in relation to number three, and number three in relation to number two. Who comes first?

That is the main idea. I move from the order of responsibility, in which even what isn't my business is my business, from mercy, to justice, which limits that initial priority of the other that we started out from.

To get back to my question on the relation to the other, you write that 'the relations with alterity stand in contrast to those in which the same dominates or absorbs or envelops the other.' What is alterity really about?

In that relation to the other, there is no fusion: the relation to the other is envisioned as alterity. The other is alterity. Buber's thought prompted me to engage in a phenomenology of sociality, which is more than the human. Sociality, for me, is the best of the human. It is the good, and not the second best to an impossible fusion. In the alterity of the face, the for-the-other commands the *I*. Ultimately it is a question of founding the justice that offends the face on the obligation with respect to the face; the extraordinary exteriority of the face.

Sociality is that alterity of the face, of the for-the-other that calls out to me, a voice that rises within me before all verbal expression, in the mortality of the *I*, from the depths of my weakness. That voice is an order. I have the order to answer for the life of

103

the other person. I do not have the right to leave him alone to his death.

The access to the face is lived in the ethical mode. The face, all by itself, has a meaning. What does it offer to my gaze? What does it say?

The face is a seigniory and defenselessness itself. What does the face say when I approach it? That face, exposed to my look, is disarmed. Whatever countenance it may put on, whether this face belongs to an important person, titled, or in appearance simpler. This face is the same, exposed in its nakedness. Beneath the countenance it gives itself, all its weakness comes through, and at the same time its mortality emerges; to the point where I can want to liquidate it entirely. Why not? But that is where all ambiguity of the face, and of the relation to the other, lies. This face of the other, without recourse, without security, exposed to my look and in its weakness and its mortality is also the one that orders me: 'Thou shalt not kill.' There is, in the face, the supreme authority that commands, and I always say it is the word of God. The face is the locus of the word of God. There is the word of God in the other, a non-thematized word.

The face is that possibility of murder, that powerlessness of being and that authority that commands me: 'Thou shalt not kill.'

So what distinguishes the face in its status from all

known objects comes from its contradictory nature. It is all weakness and all authority.

That order that it exposes to the other also comes from the requirement of responsibility on my part. That infinite, in a sense, that gives itself to me, marks a non-indifference for me in my relation to the other, in which I am never done with him. When I say 'I am doing my duty' I lie, because I am never discharged with respect to the other. And in this 'never released,' there is the *'mise-en-scène'* of the infinite, an inexhaustible, concrete responsibility. The impossibility of saying no.

But it is that anarchy that makes me say 'Here I am,' or 'Send me' toward the other. A responsibility never discharged, and always once again future, which is not to come, but supervenes.[1] A responsibility prior to deliberation, to which I was exposed, dedicated, before being dedicated to myself.

You write: 'I am for myself solely to the degree that I am responsible,' but you go still further, since you express the I as hostage for the widow, the indigent and the orphan. This I, who is addressed – is he not primarily the hostage to any face that is presented to it?

That way of being for the other, i.e., of being responsible for the other, is something dreadful, because it means that if the other does something I am the one who is responsible. The hostage is the one who is found responsible for what he has not done.

105

The one responsible for the wrongdoing of the other. I am responsible in principle, and I am so before the justice that distributes, before the measures of justice. It is concrete, you know! It is not made up! When you have encountered a human being, you cannot drop him. Most often we do so, saying 'I have done all I could!' We haven't done anything! It is this feeling, this consciousness, of having done nothing that gives us the status of hostage with the responsibility of one who is not guilty, who is innocent. The innocent, what a paradox! That is one who does no harm. It is the one who pays for the other.

The other involves us in a situation in which we are obligated without guilt, but our obligation is no less for that. At the same time it is a burden. It is heavy, and, if you like, that is what goodness is.

The trace of the infinite is inscribed in my obligation toward the other, in this moment that corresponds to the call.

You just mentioned goodness. That is not philosophical language, but still! I know that you are overwhelmed by Vasily Grossman in his book Life and Fate. *Could you talk to us about it?*

That book describes the situation in Europe during the time of Stalin and Hitler. Vasily Grossman represents that society as being completely dehumanized. There is the life in the camps, of course; it was the same thing under Hitler and Stalin. Life seems regulated on the basis of total contempt for the human person, lack of respect for man; but as for Stalin, that society is the outcome of the quest for a liberated humanity. The circumstances of Marxism's having turned into Stalinism is the greatest offence to the cause of the human, because Marxism bore the hopes of humanity: it may be one of the greatest psychological shocks for the twentieth-century European. Those 800 pages offer a complete spectacle of desolation and dehumanization. The book reflects absolute despair, and I see no horizon, no salvation for the human race.

But in the decay of human relations, in that sociological misery, goodness persists. In the relation of one person to another person, goodness is possible. There is a long monologue in which Ikonnikov, the character who expresses the author's ideas, puts all social preachments in doubt. That is, all rational organization with an ideology and plans. The impossibility of goodness as a government, as a social institution. Every attempt to organize the human fails. The only thing that remains vigorous is the goodness of everyday life. Ikonnikov calls it the little goodness.

Yes indeed, this passage is very important, and with your permission I would like to quote it. Mostovkoi is in prison, and he undertakes to read the writings of Ikonnikov. He reads these words: 'Most of those being who inhabit the earth do not take as a goal the definition of

*the good.' In what does the good consist? The good is not
in nature, and it is not in the preachings of the prophets,
either, or in the great social doctrines, or in the ethics of
the philosophers. But simple people bear in their hearts
the love of all living thing; they love life naturally; they
protect life. And a bit further he adds: 'Thus there exists
side by side with this so terrible greater good human
kindness in everyday life. It is the kindness of an old lady
who gives a piece of bread to a convict along the roadside.
It is the kindness of a soldier who holds his canteen out
to a wounded enemy. The kindness of youth taking pity
on old age, the kindness of a peasant who hides an old
Jew in his barn.' And so on.*[2]

The book is frightening, and on every page that is
the only positive thing. He even specifies that that
little goodness or kindness of one for another is a
goodness without witnesses. That goodness escapes
all ideology: he says that 'it could be described as
goodness without thought.' Why without thought?
Because it is goodness outside all systems, all religions,
all social organizations. Gratuitous, that goodness is
eternal.

It is the feeble-minded who defend it and work at
its perpetuation from one being to another. It is so
fragile before the might of evil. Grossman writes that
it is as if all the simple-minded tried to douse the
worldwide conflagration with a syringe.

This book leaves us in an awkward position. For
despite all the horrors man has brought about, that

poor kindness holds on. It is a 'mad goodness,' the most human thing there is in man. It defines man, despite its powerlessness, and Ikonnikov has another beautiful image to qualify it: 'It is beautiful and powerless, like the dew.' What freshness in this despair!

But it is true that the moment this goodness organizes it goes out. Despite the rottenness, the magnitude of evil wrought in the name of the good, the human subsists in that form of one for the other, in the relation of one to the other. The other as face, extraordinary testimony to my freedom, who commands me alterity in the infinite, who elects me to its service and who represents the ethical disturbance of being and is going to lead it [being] along the pathway of ethical dis-interestedness. The coming of the human to ethics passes through this ethical suffering, the disturbance brought by every face, even in an ordered world.

This saintliness of the human cannot be expressed on the basis of any category. Are we entering a moment in history in which the good must be loved without promises? Perhaps it is the end of all preaching. May we not be on the eve of a new form of faith, a faith without triumph, as if the only irrefutable value were saintliness, a time when the only right to a reward would be not to expect one?

The first and last manifestation of God would be to be without promises.

7

Utopia and Socialism

The condemnation of Stalinism by the very society it wrought marked the end of a certain idea of doctrinal infallibility that had settled into people's minds. Socialist certainty, which until recently had remained direct and dogmatic, and impressed even its adversaries by its power of expansion, is now in search of a more critical and more difficult assurance. In its faithfulness to Marxism, which, as one cannot forget, was able to transform concepts into movements, the search for new syntheses is beginning to make itself felt. A deepening, which is not achieved in libraries. Various rumblings have been heard over the last decade from the most well established nations. The appearance of groups and small bands who claim to be as knowledgeable as the organized and experienced large revolutionary parties, and who, in the name of new or renewed insights assume the right to act by spreading violence in the guise of abortive revolutions – that is the new spectacle of the social struggle. At times it seems to mask a sadness, a sadness that hovers over a world that has lost the security of the orthodoxies that had, up to that point, been confirmed by a rectilinear history of validating a way of thinking without afterthoughts. Disarray, but also hope! The teachings, or at least the problems, of the masters of socialism qualified as utopian – Saint-Simon, Fourrier, Proudhon, perhaps Fourrier most of all – again attract attention.

Utopian socialism: it did not yet know that the 'transformation of civilization,' as Fourrier called it, is not possible with ideas that come to you from who knows where, that it cannot do without the science that, in the structures buried within the real, present social order, can read the intentions of the future already sketched out; but a socialist mode of thought that, by its very utopianism, is capable, in its 'nostalgia for justice,' of a certain audacity of Hope, and that supplies realist action with the norms necessary for critique.

Martin Buber's book on utopian socialism, which has just been translated by Paul Corset and François Girard, completed in 1945, published in Hebrew in 1946 and in German in 1950, preceded de-Stalinisation. But it cannot leave today's reader indifferent. Buber, in his description of utopian socialism, attempts to bring out in Marxism and Leninism themselves – to which more than a quarter of the work is devoted – the involuntary or unconscious element of utopianism. The latter would be congenital to socialist thought, which is inevitably of the ethical order: prophetic and messianic. Utopianism, according to Buber at least, is – in a world in which the eschatological sense has been lost since the

Enlightenment and the French Revolution – the only way to wish for a 'completely other' society. It would be fitting to point out the similarity between this recourse to utopia and the one (differing in that it comes from the very heart of Marxism, however) perceived or postulated by Ernst Bloch: the referral of all attempts to regenerate man to a radical renewal, to what *is* not yet at all, to an unreality more unreal, so to speak, than the social future discernable in the factual present, to the 'principle of hope' that, if we are to believe Ernst Bloch, is civilization itself, through the prophets, philosophers and artists.

If we consider Buber's work as an essay on the history of ideas, his account of utopian socialism, from Saint-Simon to Kropotkin and Landauer, might require some supplement in the area of influences undergone and exerted, and as to the completeness of the systems themselves. But Buber warns us already in the preface that he is leaving many developments aside. He is following an idea: it is within the opposition between the political and the social that he situates the doctrines he studies. To him, the issue seems to be to challenge the subordination of *civil society* to the State, in which, for Hegel, humanity would attain universality of thought and will, i.e., freedom. It is the idea of domination, coercion – or as we would say today, repression – that is the starting point for Buber's thinking on political relationships between men. The social, on the other hand, would signify the 'common life of man,' their

113

camaraderie, the *presence* of man to man, his proximity. Socialism would consist in the regeneration of the 'cells' of the social tissue, broken down by politics. Whence the importance given to the diverse forms and modalities of that coexistence and of cooperation: in work, production and exchange. Whence the care that there be numerous social exchange groups, in order for the presence of persons to other persons to be a 'real presence.' Whence the decentralization of the whole, to avoid the organization and the administration's intervening to 'statify' that *being-together* of men, organizing it according to abstract rules, and in the name of anonymous powers. The idea of an administration in which command is limited to the technically necessary is distinguished from governmental administration, in which the power of men over men goes beyond these necessities, in which man dominates man, and consequently in which the communitarian ends of the group are forgotten.

Aren't Marxism and Leninism mistrustful of the State to the highest degree? The division of society into classes and the domination of one class by the other, against which the proletariats unite, are the reason or secret of State. A classless society ends political powers, substitutes an administration for the government, and perfects society. Isn't that why the *soviets* – councils springing up on the spot for professional cooperation and communal life – appeared to Lenin, precisely for that reason, suited to taking over where the State leaves off? The political structures that were introduced during the Revolution, however, were only accepted as provisional, pending the coming of the new society. Buber shows how the realization of socialist society in Russia was from the beginning – and constantly – at odds with these political structures that sprang up and defeated the decentralization of the soviets. But one may wonder whether the withering away of the State is not permanently postponed in this way.

There is one lone, unique example of a socialist society that was successfully realized: collective farms – *Kibbutzim* – on the soil of the land of Israel. Buber analyzes their structure and meaning in some particularly interesting pages. (Nevertheless, on this point, we would like to have been able to measure the distance we have traversed, both before and since, and the shifting relationships over the last thirty years.) But the Kibbutzim themselves are qualified by Buber as *non-failures* rather than successes.

Thus there is, in Buber's view, a fearsome dialectic between society and the State. Rather than being the simple effect of the abuses of the powers, are not crises part of the very essence of the collective body? It is a question, and a pessimistic note in this whole recollection of socialist utopianism, and of socialism *tout court*.

Or perhaps this recollection, the ever-renewed quest for a society in which the *being-together* of men should be realized, a resistance to the forgetting of this utopian *should-be* at the very heart of State structures setting themselves up as ends in themselves, and the resurgence of conscience against the State's deterioration of social relations – are themselves objective events. Events that mark, in the society-State dialectic, the moment of morality limiting politics – an indispensable and unforgettable moment. The radical way Buber approaches the theme of political domination recalls, at times, the one so much discussed today that it has become a commonplace: the theme of the diffuse circulation of *powers*, which marks the intersubjective experiences that appear the most innocent and natural with the *will to power*. It is a situation in which men, unbeknownst to themselves, are all either dominators or dominated; a situation that, in reaction, invites us to purify all human relations of that political perversion and in which socialism appears as a new ethics! In the presence of certain acts of resistance and martyrdom, daringly carried out in our world in the name of the pure human, the utopian human, against the efficacy of powers and powerful political entities, that ethics affirms its objective status, shows itself to be *Wirklichkeit*, efficient reality, and no longer lets itself be repressed among the powerless 'beautiful souls' or 'unhappy consciousnesses.'

In any case, that would be, beyond the contribution of utopian socialism analyzed by Buber, *the credo* of his own philosophical anthropology, in which the relation of man to his neighbour is conceived of on the famous model of 'I and Thou,' distinct from the objectification and the domination that always triumphs in the eyes of the objective gaze. The 'I-Thou' model allows us to conceptualize a firm distinction between society and the State, and to conceive of a society without 'powers.' Due to a certain sense of decorum, that anthropology remains implicit throughout the pages of this work, the style itself of which, perfectly neutral and impassive – the university style – is so little reminiscent of Buber's ardent and 'inspired' style. But the present essay may be considered a sociological – and immediately socialist – prolongation of that anthropology.

III

PEACE AND RIGHT

8

The Prohibition against Representation and 'The Rights of Man'

In memory of Adélie Rassial

Is the 'prohibition against representation' (which, by the way, applies only to certain images in the Jewish tradition[1]) to be understood in the limited sense of a religious rule, and a purely repressive one at that? The intent, in raising this question, is certainly not to undervalue the pedagogical importance of such a restriction, i.e., to overlook its contribution to the 'spirituality' of a mode of thought ascending from the useful to the gracious, and from the sacred to the holy, that I admire in Judaism. And even there, to gauge that importance accurately and fairly within Jewish piety and sensibility, one would have to go back to its scriptural sources. 'Prohibition against representation': we should not allow that expression to circulate glibly and out of context, like an aphorism, without having previously examined closely what the written Law of the Bible says about it, and, in its multidimensional and multilevel language, the oral Law of the Talmud, in which, moreover, all representation is authorized when it is a question of scientific research.[2] A study requiring considerable erudition and a learned hermeneutics. Was it undertaken by those who have spoken before me? I hope so. That is not my purpose.

As for me, I would like to inquire into whether, beneath the mistrust of images of beings recommended by Jewish monotheism, there is not a denunciation, in the structures of signifying and the meaningful, of a certain favoring of representation over other possible modes of thought. In representation – *cogitatio et cogitatum* – presence is created and recreated, i.e., the presentation and the alterity of a *cogitatum*, but, and precisely to the same degree, an auto-donation or a giving-itself-over to thought. Whence an offering-itself to a taking. And thus, in the concreteness that is indispensable to a phenomenological description, can one fail to notice an offering-itself to hands already outstretched? And further, can one fail to include, in the taking-in-hand, the *a priori* of a latent incarnation of thought, and in that taking, forget the taken: a solid, a being, a thing, or 'something'? Cohesion and complicity of a seeing and a taking, but, in the re-presentation, the putting of that which is thought [*le pensé*] at the disposal of, and *on the same scale* as, thinking [*la pensée*]: a deep-seated immanence or atheism in sight and knowledge, or their temptation to idolatry! Here we have thought, approaching even the uniqueness of the unique that is expressed in the face, in the same way as visible and plastic forms. Uniqueness of the *one of a kind* –

or uniqueness having broken with all kinds – in the sense of the loved one being unique for the one who loves. A uniqueness that, to the one who loves, immediately means fear for the death of the loved one. Now, in the image, thought reaches the face of the other reduced to its plastic forms, exalted, fascinating, and proceeding from an exacerbated imagination though they may be. Though they may be a work of art!

From a certain point of view, in the plasticity of pure appearance, there emerges the caricature of 'eyes that do not see,' 'ears that do not hear,' 'noses that do not smell' of *Psalms* 115. We catch a glimpse of an inanimate idol in these verses, but especially the inanimate resembling the face, which allows itself to be 'portrayed,' to go into 'copies,' 'exempla': shadows that destroy the uniqueness of the unique and return it – an individual – to the generality, the extension of a genus. Opening of the very 'order' in which resemblance reigns or is disseminated.

Representation comes down to a thinking of this or that, to an intentionality, a thematization of what puts itself forward or gives itself in presence or representation, of what lets itself be designated – ultimately or immediately – by a demonstrative, and in a word concretely, with the index finger. Thus a thought thinking the thing prevails.[3] The latter is not a real part of that thought, but, in presence, it is given to that thought. An 'unreally' or ideally present thing, present in the guise of 'intentional object,' according to the Husserlian terminology: present to thought, without in any way being a real part of that thought. But it is present with a presence that contracts and fixes with certainty the logical articulations, the empty forms of thought, which gathers itself in them, into thematization and knowledge. These forms espouse even the conceptual, though it is already so far from the sensible, but is still taken as *etwas überhaupt*, which in French is expressed so admirably as *'quelque chose'* [some thing], revealing, in the empty form so named, as in the vestiges of a thing.

This empty form is applied to time itself, thought of as *presence*, right down to the consciousness of its 'flow,' of its dia-chrony, immediately interpreted on the basis of a re-tained or pro-tained, remembered or anticipated presence, as synchronization of duration in representation, or as a historical account in the simultaneity of writing symbols gathered into a text that encompasses and unites temporal periods. A time whose diachrony is thus lived as a 'privation' of immobile eternity, and expressed by the metaphor of flux, as if time were a *being [étant]*, comparable to a flowing liquid. There is a privilege granted to the 'something' in thought which is also indicated by the resources of language, in which all signification can be expressed as a noun in a statement, in which all signification can become a substantive, whatever the native or primitive grammatical category may be: adjective, verb, adverb, preposition, conjunction or interjection, and all the syntactic particles, and all the components of the sentence, and the sentence, the full assertion.

Given this, may not the 'prohibition against representation' be the denunciation of an *intelligibility* that one would like to reduce to knowledge, and that pretends to be original or ultimate, claiming, wrongly perhaps, the dignity of being the birthplace of, and bearer of, the indelible categories of the mind? Doubtless no one would be ridiculous or foolish enough to question the legitimacy and sovereignty of knowledge and the substantive in an indispensable domain and at an essential moment of the intelligence. In the 'prohibition against representation' I am only questioning the exclusive privilege that Western culture has conferred on consciousness [*conscience*] and the science [*science*] it carries within itself, and that, as self-consciousness, promises ultimate wisdom and absolute thought.

The reason this question arises is certainly not because representation would be dedicated exclusively to the pure materiality of the thing, as if it were incapable of abstraction and could not intend the non-material. It is rather because, in the presence that it does not cease renewing, the adequation of thought with its other is always accomplished; because as intentionality it always intends 'something': a goal, an end, a finite thing, term. Is all thought nothing but aim and intentionality, finality, and a hold on the finite? The challenging of intentionality does not tend to return to a psyche closed in on itself, in some

125

sensible impression, in which sensualist empiricism or psychological atomism was content. The prohibition against representation would on the contrary suggest in the meaningful a transcendence in comparison to which that of intentionality was but an internment within self-consciousness, though it is less narrow and unbreathable than the immanence of the sensation in Condillac.

This transcendence is alive in the relation to the other man, i.e. in the proximity of one's fellow man, whose *uniqueness* and consequently whose irreducible *alterity* would be – still or already – unrecognized in the perception that stares at [*dé-visage*] the other. Beneath the plasticity of the face [*figure*] that *appears*, the face [*visage*] is already missed. It is frozen in art itself, despite the artist's possible attempt to disfigure the 'something' that starts again, figurative, in presence. Transcendence of the other man in his face, in his *facing-up-to* [*faire face*] which in its extreme *directness* (original concreteness of all directness) is an exposure to inexorable death. Before all particular expression and beneath every particular expression (which already, pose and countenance that one gives oneself – which already, grimace, covers and protects), there is a stripping bare and a nakedness of expression as such, defenseless nakedness, extradition to death, precariousness more precarious than any precariousness in that directness of exposure. Face as mortality, mortality of the other beyond his appearing; nakedness more naked, so to speak, than that which the unveiling of truth exposes: beyond the visibility of the phenomenon, a victim's abandonment. But in that very precariousness, the 'Thou shalt not kill' that is also the meaning of the face; in that *directness* of exposure, the proclamation – before any verbal sign – of a right that peremptorily calls upon my responsibility for the other man. It assigns me and demands me, as if the invisible death which the face of the other faces – uniqueness separated from any whole – were *my business*. Some of the very ego-ness of the *I* in that non-transferable responsibility, like an election instituting the *I* as a uniqueness. Responsibility deriving from no guilt; a gratuitous responsibility responding to a commandment not to leave the other alone in his or her last extremity, as if the death of the other, before being my death, concerned me; as if in that death – invisible to the other who is exposed to it – I became by my indifference the accomplice while I could do something about it. Would not the tranquility and good conscience of perseverance in being be the equivalent here of letting the other man die? 'Thou shalt not kill' – that means then 'Thou shalt cause thy neighbour to live.' Event of sociality prior to all association in the name of an abstract and common 'humanity.' *The right of man, absolutely and originally*, takes on meaning only in the other, as the right of the other man. A right with respect to which I am never released! Hence infinite responsibility for the other: the radical impossibility of immanence! An affinity that 'comes to mind' in the silent command of the face. The word of God? In any case, the one that must *precede* Revelation in the positive religions if the men who listen for it want to know who is addressing them, and to recognize a voice they have already heard. Of course it is obviously true that the relation to the other can also be described as approaching someone taken as a number in a totality of a genus (taken as a 'something'), and that one can 'experience' the other, seize his or her thoughts and inner life and self, making them enter into a calculus or a politics, on the basis of that person's expressive gestures and words, by analogy with those the observer knows of his own (the observer, the man assured of his own right to be), and that this can suffice for both his day-to-day behavior and his attitude toward the future and history, to his way of managing amidst represented things and persons. In this scheme of things, the other man, the neighbour, will already have compromised or enervated the radical alterity of his uniqueness itself, facilitating the administration and statistics necessary for the economic, military and technical equilibrium of totally represented being. And indeed to the extent that that equilibrium makes it possible to respond better, with responsibly for the other, to the right of man (which is originally the right of the *other man*), that universal representation cannot be forbidden. But it is the epiphany of the face that, before any particular expression, uniqueness or alterity is expressed, which is refractory to the image, to the consciousness of . . ., and its 'transcendental synthesis.' It is there that an 'unheard of command,' or 'the word of God' is heard; it interrupts the unity of the 'I think' in each person who, unique, is awakened to a non-transferable responsibility for the first person who comes along. A gratuitous responsibility: independent of what I may or may not have committed. The non-transferable responsibility of my logically indiscernible uniqueness. Responsibility which is also the stern name of love without lust.

It is the decisive ideas of Husserl on *Gebrauchsobjecte* – objects of use, our 'things,' irreducible to their purely theoretical appearance, and having 'constitutively,' qua objects of use, the same immediacy as the presence of what Husserl calls *Vorhandene Objecte als solche*[4] – ideas that, in the brilliant analysis in *Sein und Zeit* lead to the notion of 'utensility' (or of Heidegger's *Zuhandenheit*) understood as a way of being freed from all 'foundation' in any sort of 'objectivity,' or pre-existing *Vorhandenheit* available to a 'plain seeing' (*bloßes Hinsehen*); ideas that remain foreign to the ethical problem proper, and in which we heard, very early on, the echo of Bergson's proposition: 'To recognize an object is to know how to use it,' and also the reverberations of all that, in Lucien Lévy-Bruhl's work, was taught on representation in 'primitive mentality'[5] ... it is certainly all these views that encouraged me to reflect on thought freed of all representation. (And this, prior to any contact, in this regard, with the admirable teachings

129

of Buber and Gabriel Marcel, to whom are indebted all who, even without realizing it, have trod the soil cleared by them.) All these pages, which suggest a *meaningfulness* prior to representation, in which transcendental philosophy situated the origin of thought, have enabled us to hear, behind the already plastic forms in which the face does no more than present itself, re-present itself and appear as an image, and where, in that image, the face reveals itself as *some thing* – all those pages enabled us to hear (so to speak) the ancient, biblical call and command that awakens the subject to a responsibility for the other on the basis of an uprightness [*droiture*] that is exposure to death. Mortality, but also a right that challenges the *I*, substantial and persevering remorselessly in its being, that Pascal called hateful.

9

Peace And Proximity

I

The problem of Europe and peace is precisely the one posed by the contradiction of our European consciences. It is the problem of humanity in us, of the centrality the Europe whose 'vital forces' – those in which the brutal perseverance of beings in their being – are already seduced by peace, by peace preferred to violence, and, more precisely still, by the peace of a humanity that, European in us, has already decided in favor of the Greek wisdom, which is to await human peace on the basis of Truth. Peace on the basis of truth, which (marvel of marvels) commands men without forcing or combating them, which governs or assembles them without making them subservient, which can convince [*convaincre*] them with words without conquering [*vaincre*] them, and which masters nature's hostile elements by the calculations and practical knowledge of technology. Peace on the basis of the State, which is the gathering together of men participating in the same ideal truths. A peace that is enjoyed therein as tranquillity assured by solidarity – the exact measure of reciprocity in services rendered between counterparts: the unity of a

Whole in which each finds his or her rest, place or basis. Peace as tranquillity or rest! The peace of rest between beings having a firm footing or resting on the underlying solidity of their substance, self-sufficient in their identity or capable of satisfying themselves seeking satisfaction.

But the conscience of Europe is a bad conscience, because of the contradiction that tears her apart at the very hour of her modernity, which is probably that of ledgers set up in lucidity, that of full consciousness. That history of a peace, a freedom and well-being promised on the basis of a light that a universal knowledge projected on the world and human society – even unto the religious messages that sought justification for themselves in the truths of knowledge – that history is not recognizable in its millennia of fratricidal struggles, political or bloody, of imperialism, scorn and exploitation of the human being, down to our century of world wars, the genocides of the Holocaust and terrorism; unemployment and continual desperate poverty of the Third World; ruthless doctrines and cruelty of fascism and national socialism, right down to the supreme paradox of the defense of man and his rights being perverted into Stalinism.

Hence the challenge to centrality of Europe and its culture. A worn-out Europe! The shattering of the universality of theoretical reason, which arose betimes in the 'Know thyself,' and sought the entire universe within self-consciousness. Hence the affirmation and championing of specific cultures in all corners of the globe. An affirmation that found support and thanks – and often its origin – and always sympathetic understanding – at the highest levels of the European university itself. An interest on the part of our old world, in the name of the ancient universalism of Europe itself, for the countless particularisms that pretend to be its equal. An interest that no longer stems from some taste for 'barbaric exoticism,' but the exaltation of a logic *other* than that of Aristotle, of a thought other than civilized. An exaltation that may be explainable as remorse fed by the memory of colonial wars and the long oppression of those once called savages, a long indifference to the sadness of a whole world. Hence the challenge to the centrality of Europe by Europe itself. But perhaps in that very challenge there is the testimony of a Europe that is not just Hellenic! And hence also the question as to what, precisely, the role of this latter is, in a Europe that one would wish faithful to all its promises.

Europe against Europe, in yet another aspect and in relation to the most dramatic eventualities. The great empires that, to such a great extent, decide the fate of our planet, are the product of a European politics, economy, science and technology, and their power of expansion. Universalism or imperialism! European empires overflowing geographical Europe and vying in power to the point of preparing – if necessary – to blow up the very earth that bears humanity. The explosion of the earth itself by an energy that the search for truth – having become modern science – released from being. Here we have truth threatening being itself. Here truth threatens, so to speak, being qua being and disqualifies Europe, which discovered – and left uncovered – these forces. But doubtless that very way of disqualifying and accusing already proceeds from a vocation of the spirit whose powers of love are neither translated nor exhausted by the love of wisdom.

II

That bad conscience expresses more than just a contradiction between a certain project of culture and its results. It is not made up solely of the seductions of a peace that ensures to each person the tranquillity of his happiness and a freedom to own the world, and also, no doubt, even the possibility of owning, which nothing would disturb. It is not the failure of a speculative or dialectical project in the Hegelian style, a project that is indifferent to wars and assassinations and suffering, as long as they are necessary in the unfolding of rational thought, which is also a politics – as long as they are necessary in the formation of concepts, the logic and rational completion of which are all that matter. It is not the intellectual disappointment of a system belied by the incoherence of reality that is the drama of Europe. Nor even just the danger of dying, which is frightening to each one of us. There is the anguish of committing crimes even where concepts are in agreement. There is the anguish of the responsibility incumbent upon each one of us in the death or suffering of the other. The fear of each for himself in the mortality of each does not succeed in *absorbing* the gravity of the murder committed and the scandal of indifference to the other's suffering. Behind the risk run by each for himself in a world without security looms the consciousness of the immediate immorality of a culture and a history. Have we not heard, in the vocation of Europe, before the message of truth that it bears, the 'Thou shalt not kill' of the Decalogue and the Bible? In *Genesis* 32, Jacob is troubled at the news that his brother Esau – enemy or friend – is marching to meet him 'at the head of four hundred men.' Verse 8 informs us: 'Jacob was greatly afraid and anguished.'[1] What is the difference between fear and anguish? Rashi, the famous Rabbinical commentator, specifies: He was fearful for his death, but anguished at possibly having to kill.

Reflecting on this ethical moment of our European crisis – reflecting on our anguish (the anguish of Jacob, felt at the prospect of violence to be committed, even if it was necessary to the logical unfolding of history, even if it was necessary to the unfolding ordered by the march of truth advancing in absolute thought and promising at the end of the road the peace of 'the identity of the identical and the non-identical') – reflecting on this ethical moment of our European crisis (attested in particular by the philo-

135

sophical work of a Franz Rosenzweig, reared in Hegelian thought, but experiencing the First World War, though only the First), we may wonder whether peace must not respond to a call more urgent than that of truth and initially distinct from the call of truth. One may wonder whether one should not construe the ideal of truth itself – which no European can gainsay – already as subordinate to an ideal of peace that, older than that of knowledge, will but open itself to the call of truth; one may wonder whether knowledge itself and the politics governing history do not find their proper place in already responding to the requirement of peace and let themselves be guided by that requirement. But peace in this case will no longer be reducible to a simple confirmation of human identity in its substantiality, anchored in itself, in its identity of *I*. It will no longer be a question of the bourgeois peace of the man who is at home behind closed doors, rejecting that which, being exterior, negates him. It will no longer be peace in conformity with the ideal of *the unity of the One* that all alterity disturbs. In a sensibility in which the scandal of murder is not suppressed even when the violence is rationally necessary, peace cannot mean the serene tranquillity of the identical, nor can alterity be justified solely as the logical distinction of parts *belonging to a fractured whole*, united into a whole by rigorously reciprocal relations.

Precisely what must be challenged is the conception according to which, in the human multiplicity, the *I* would be reduced to a fraction of a Whole, which is reconstituted in its solidarity after the manner of an organism, or a concept, the unity of which is the coherence of members or the structure of an understanding. The question must be asked (and this is the other term of an alternative) apropos of the identity of the *I* – whether the alterity of the other does not have, *from the start*, the character of an absolute, in the etymological sense of the term; as if the other were not other just in the logical sense, other by a logically surmountable alterity in a common *genus*, or transcendentally surmountable, lending itself to the synthesis carried out by a Kantian 'I think.' We must ask ourselves whether peace, instead of consisting in the absorption or the disappearance of alterity, would not on the contrary be the *fraternal* way of a proximity to the other, which would not be simply the failure of coincidence with the other, but which would signify precisely the *excess* of sociality over all solitude – excess of sociality and love. I do not pronounce this often misused word lightly.

Peace as relation with an alterity, irreducible to a common genus in which, already contained in a logical community, it would be only a relative alterity. Peace thus independent of all appurtenance to a system, irreducible to a totality and as if refractory to synthesis. The project of a peace different from the political peace discussed above. An ethical relation that would thus not be a simple deficiency or privation of the unity of the One reduced to the multi-

plicity of individuals in the extension of the genus!
Here, on the contrary, in ethical peace, a relation to
the inassimilable other, the irreducible other, the
unique other. Only the unique is irreducible and
absolutely other!

But the uniqueness of the unique is the uniqueness
of the beloved. The uniqueness of the unique signifies
in love. Hence peace as love. Not that the uniqueness
of alterity is conceived of as some subjective illusion
of a lover. Quite to the contrary, the *subjective* as such
is precisely the penetration – through the impassive
essence [*essence*] of being [*être*] and the rigor of its
logical forms and genera, and through the violence of
its perseverance in being – toward the unique, the
absolutely other, by love, proximity and peace. A
proximity different than some 'short distance' measured in geometrical space, separating some from
others. A peace different than the simple unity of the
diverse in a synthesis integrating them. Peace as a
relation with the other in his logically indiscernible
alterity, in his alterity irreducible to the logical identity of an ultimate difference added to a genus. Peace
as the incessant awakening to that alterity and to that
uniqueness. Proximity as the impossible assumption
of difference, impossible definition, impossible integration. Proximity as impossible appearance. But
proximity! Husserl's famous 'appresentation,' not at
all as an impoverished representation, but as the
mysterious excess of the beloved. The excellence
proper of transcendence without reference to the

138

immanence of the true, which in the West passes for the supreme grace of the spiritual. Indeed it is obvious that it is in the knowledge of the other as a simple individual – the individual of a genus, a class, a race – that peace with the other changes into hatred; it is the approach to the other as a 'kind of this or that.'

III

I have not conducted this formal analysis of peace – as *relation* with the unique and the other – a relation designated by the general term of love – without trying to deformalize, to recover these structures in their concreteness, without a phenomenology. I have thought that the uniqueness and the alterity of the unique is concretely the face of the other man, the original epiphany of which is not in its visibility as a plastic form, but in 'appresentation.' The thought awakened to the face of the other man is not a thought of . . ., a representation, but from the start a thought for . . ., a non-indifference for the other, breaking the equilibrium of the even and impassive soul of pure knowledge, an awakening to the other man in his uniqueness indiscernible for knowledge, an approach to the first one to come along in his proximity as neighbour and unique one. Face, before any particular expression and beneath all expression that – already countenance given to self – hides the nakedness of the face. Face that is not unveiling but pure denudation of defenseless exposure. Exposure as

139

such, extreme exposure to the precariousness of the stranger. Nakedness of pure exposure that is not simply emphasis of the known, of the unveiled in truth: exposure that is expression, a first language, call and assignation.

Face that thus is not exclusively the face of man. In Vasily Grossman's *Life and Fate* (Part Three, Chapter 23), there is mention of a visit to the Lubianka in Moscow by the families or wives or relatives of political prisoners, to get news of them. A line is formed in front of the windows, in which they can only see each other's backs. A woman waits for her turn: 'Never had she thought the human back could be so expressive and transmit states of mind so penetratingly. The people who approached the window had a special way of stretching the neck and back; the raised shoulders had shoulder-blades tensed as if by springs, and they seemed to shout, to cry, to sob.' Face as the extreme precariousness of the other. Peace as awakening to the precariousness of the other.

For in that extreme uprightness of the face and in its expression, assignation and demand that concern the *I*, that concern *me*. In that extreme uprightness [*droiture*], his right [*droit*] over me. The demand that concerns me as *I* is the concrete circumstance in which the right signifies. As if the invisible death that the other faces were *my* business, as if that death concerned me. In this calling back to responsibility of the *I* by the face that assigns, demands and claims it, the other is the neighbour.

Taking as our starting point that uprightness of the face of the other, I once wrote that the face of the other in its precariousness and defenselessness is for me both the temptation to kill and the call for peace, the 'Thou shalt not kill.' Face that already accuses me, is suspicious of me, but already claims and demands me. The right of man is there, in that uprightness of exposure and command and assignation, a right older than any conferring of honor and any merit. The proximity of the neighbour – the peace of proximity – is the responsibility of the *I* for the other, the impossibility of leaving him alone before the mystery of death. Which, concretely, is the taking up of dying for the other. Peace with the other goes even unto this. It is all the gravity of the love of one's neighbour, of love without lust.

Peace of the love of one's neighbour in which it is not a question, as in the peace of pure repose, of confirming oneself in one's identity, but of putting that identity itself in question, its unlimited freedom and its power.

IV

But the order of truth and knowledge has a role to play in that peace of proximity and in the ethical order it signifies. To a very great extent, it is the ethical order of human proximity that brings about or summons that of objectivity, truth and knowledge. This is very important to the very meaning of

Europe: its biblical heritage implies the necessity of the Greek heritage. Europe is not a simple confluence of two cultural currents. It is the concretization in which the wisdoms of the theoretical and the biblical do better than converge. The relation with the other and the unique, which is peace, comes to require a reason that thematizes and synchronizes and synthesizes, that thinks the world and reflects on being; concepts necessary to the peace of men.

Responsibility for the other man is, in its immediacy, certainly prior to all questions. But how does it oblige, if a third party disturbs that exteriority of two people, in which my subjection qua subject is a subjection to my neighbour? The third party is other than the neighbour, but also another neighbour, and also a neighbour of the other, and not just his counterpart [*semblable*]. What am I to do? What have they already done to one another? Which one comes before the other in my responsibility? What are they, then, the other and the third party, in relation to one another? Birth of the question.

The first question in the inter-human is the question of justice. Henceforth it becomes necessary to know, to make oneself a conscience. To my relation with the *unique* and the incomparable, comparison is superimposed, and, with a view to equity or equality, a weighing, a calculation, the comparison of incomparables, and therewith neutrality – presence or representation – of being, the thematization and visibility of the face, discountenanced [*dévisagé*] in a manner of

142

speaking as the simple individuation of the individual; the weight of having and of exchanges; the necessity of thinking together beneath one synthetic theme the multiple and the unity of the world; and thereby the promotion of the relation and ultimate signifyingness of being to intentional and intelligible thought; and finally thereby the extreme importance in human multiplicity of the political structure of society under the rule of law, and hence institutions in which the *for-the-other* of subjectivity – in which the *I* – enters with the dignity of the citizen into the perfect reciprocity of political laws that are essentially egalitarian or held to become so.

But the forms of the spirit thus promoted and the notions such as being or rational truth that thus take on the character of being originary of all meaning, and the political unity with the institution and the relations that are instituted on that basis are, at every moment, on the verge of bearing within themselves their center of gravity and of weighing in their own right on the fate of men, as a source of conflict and violence. It seemed to me important, therefore, to recall peace and justice as their origin, justification and measure; to recall that that justice which can legitimize them ethically – i.e., retain the sense proper of the human as dis-inter-estedness beneath the weight of being – is not a natural and anonymous legality regulating human masses, from which a technique of social equilibrium has been derived to harmonize antagonistic, blind forces through transitional cruelty and violence, and that it is impossible to justify in such a way a State abandoned to its own necessity. Nothing can escape the control of the responsibility of 'one for the other,' which delimits the State and ceaselessly calls for the watchfulness of persons, who cannot content themselves with the simple subsuming of cases beneath the general rule, as the computer is capable of doing.

It is not unimportant to know – and this is perhaps the European experience of the twentieth century – whether the egalitarian and just State in which the European realizes himself – and that is to be instituted and preserved – proceeds from a war of all against all – or from the irreducible responsibility of one for the other, and whether it can ignore the uniqueness of the face and of love. It is not unimportant to know this, so that war does not become the institution of a war with a good conscience in the name of historical necessities. Consciousness is born as the presence of the third party in the proximity of the one to the other, and thus it is to the extent that it proceeds from it that it can become dis-inter-estedness. The foundation of consciousness is justice, and not vice-versa. Objectivity resting on justice. To the extravagant generosity of the for-the-other is superposed a reasonable, ancillary or angelic order; that of justice through knowledge, and here philosophy is a *measure* brought to the infinite of the being-for-the-other of peace and proximity, and as it were a wisdom of love.

144

10

The Rights of the Other Man

The formal characteristic of the Rights of Man, such as they are conceived of since the Renaissance, consists in their being attached to every human person independently from any prior granting by any authority or tradition, and also independently from any act of taking upon oneself or of meriting these rights. Also called natural, these rights would also belong to men equally, regardless of the physical or mental, personal or social differences that distinguish men from one another. Prior to all agreed upon law, they are *a priori*. Human beings guilty toward others, upon whose rights they infringe and who, by material or psychological incapacity, are unable to exercise these rights issued from their human nature fully in fact, are indeed subjected to a limitation of these rights by their empirical degradation. But that limitation is legitimate, so to speak, or still in conformity with the fullness of these rights, understood in the (implicit or explicit) 'judgment' in which that limitation is pronounced.

The effectiveness of the Rights of Man, their incorporation into the judicial determinism and their weight in that order, the very fact of their discovery and concrete formulation, brings with it necessary social and psychological conditions that owe much to the cultural, technical and economic state of a society – to the influence of foreign civilizations, near or far, and to the lucidity and intellectual refinement of the citizenry. These conditions are not the basis of these rights qua rights. They are neither the principle of, nor the justification for, this 'privilege,' attaching *a priori* to the human person. But the content [*teneur*] of this right is not arbitrarily invented. Does it not derive *vi formae* from the very *a priori* in which its 'normative energy' appears, in the guise of the right to *free will*, and thus as independence from an absolute, as a dignity?

But the right of man, signifying the right to a free will, is exercised in the concreteness of the empirical order of man – of man among men, in being-there – as the right to being-there or to live, and hence as the right to satisfy the needs that sustain life and as the right to work, allowing you to 'earn a living,' and as the right to well-being and to the beautiful, that makes life bearable. And why not even a right to 'weekends' and 'paid vacations' and all the benefits of Social Security? But then does not the requirement of the right of man extend across the entire field of life-in-the-world, even if it does admit of levels of urgency?

The charter of the Rights of Man would thus extend to the entire dispersion and hierarchy of human relations – direct relations, and those that are

146

established around things – and the validity of that
charter would continually clash with what we may
call the mechanical necessities of the social reality
known to the positive sciences, which are mainly
attentive to causal laws; which indicates perhaps
especially the entire extent of a purely technical task
of reforms incumbent on the defenders of the Rights
of Man. This considerable task is not reducible to the
awakening of consciousness to the Rights of Man in
the underdeveloped or tyrannized countries. It consists in establishing and formulating the requirements
of freedom and its concrete conditions in the effective
reality of modern civilization, predetermined by
physical and social mechanisms, even though the
political wisdom that that task gives rise to may have
to introduce into the rules of traditional politics and
in the play of its forces and passions a new finality of
the Rights of Man, which, since the eighteenth-
century, has learned the way of revolutionary
struggle.

But the conception of the right of man as the right
to free will – a content suggested by the form of this
right, by its *a priori* – would it not be immediately
put back in question by the coexistence and the very
multiplicity of the 'holders of rights,' who, all 'unique
and free,' would violate each other's rights or freedoms in limiting them? The war of each against all,
based on the Rights of Man! Unless we attribute to
the essence of free will a propensity for the rational,
and, thus, a respect for the universal, thanks to which

the imperative and the normative of the intelligible would impose themselves on the free will of each, consenting to limit itself in such a way as not to limit others. A limitation of its own freedom. But also a free limitation of its freedom! A free limitation, in consenting to the rationality of the universal. The consent to the reasonable would never be servitude and the will would adhere to the rational, without being subjugated to it, just like reason, which remains upright thought even as it bows to the self-evidence of the True. The respect for the other in the respectful will of the Intelligible, or, following Kant's formulation, the possibility for the will to treat the other in its decisions always as an end, or never simply as a means. To Kant, the multiplicity of free wills is reconciled in the 'Kingdom of Ends.' The peace between freedoms is thus possible, thanks to the notion of 'good will' which would be *practical reason*, a will that listens to and hears reason.

But is it certain that free will lends itself entirely to the Kantian notion of *practical reason*? Does it allow itself to be totally contained therein without raising any difficulties? Does formalism's relation to the universal appease the non-coercible part of spontaneity, which would still distinguish between the rationalism of the intellect and the rationalism that informs a will qualified as reasonable?

And *practical reason*'s intention, attributed to the will, of ensuring the right of man or the freedom of the neighbour – does it not cost free will its own right to freedom? The duty in which it would be free by virtue of the rationality of faithfulness to the maxim of action – does it not bear some submission, attested, for example, by the law itself being lived and adopted as *dura lex?* Unless a pre-eminent excellence were granted to the other *out of goodness*: unless *good will were will*, not just out of respect for the universality of a maxim of action, but out of the feeling of goodness. A simple feeling that we speak to children about, but that can have less innocent names, such as mercy or charity or love. An attachment to the other in his alterity to the point of granting him a priority over oneself. Which would doubtless mean, with respect to the 'pathological' sensibility, the pure passivity and 'heteronomy' Kant taught us to be wary of, a primordial rupture. Rupture of the human with respect to all the pre-human ontology of being persevering in its being, of the being for whom 'it is in its being only a question of that being itself.' That the Rights of Man are originally the rights of the other man, and that they express, beyond the burgeoning of identities in their own identity and their instinct for free perseverance, the *for-the-other* of the social, of the for-the-stranger – such appears to me to be the meaning of their novelty.

IV

CONVERSATIONS

11

The Philosopher and Death

It is always the living, isn't it, who speak of the dead and death: we have just repeated that. The philosophers who wonder about death do so necessarily about the death of the other, since they have no more experience of their own than do the rest of us. Even Socrates, in whose veins the hemlock poison flows as he carries on his last conversation with his disciples, who speaks of death while he is in the process of dying, has not yet lived through death itself when he speaks of it. It is Plato who will speak of the dead Socrates.

I think you have touched on an essential point here. Death is the most unknown of unknowns. It is even otherwise unknown than all unknown. It seems to me, whatever the eventual reactions of many philosophers, and even in the [general] opinion, that death is initially the nothingness of knowledge. I am not saying that it is nothingness. It is also the 'fullness' of the question, but at first: 'One does not know.' These are the first words that come [*viennent*], and they are appropriate [*conviennent*].

It is definitive disappearance, for our world. And

*with it, the speech of the one who is disappearing is
completed. One quotes the 'last words' of someone, but it
still involves words of a living person. The memoirs of
beyond the grave are also written before. The dead keep
silence.*

It is disappearance for the others. But in itself it is
the dilemma between being and the 'not to be.' The
description of the phenomenon of death is made
while one is alive. And if something happens afterward, we must admit that it is not of the order of the
experience of the living. The possibility that something happens afterward is located beyond our reach.
The idea that it involves a *tertium quid*, something
other than being and nothingness, is the very thing
that causes fright. We speak of it without ever being
sure that that is what we are talking about. It is
doubtless something that does not enter human
thought.

*And yet, death is the only point of certainty on which
thought can cast anchor, the only indubitable event of
our destiny?*

That it will come, yes. Death is the inexorable.

The only certainty, but inexorable?

All the rest is inexorable in terms of death. It is
the inexorable 'of itself,' and in this sense also the

154

frightening. What comes, and what we cannot take upon ourselves! For thought, which always moves among interdependent notions, death is the hole that undoes the system, the disturbance of all order, the dismantling of all totality. You go toward death, you 'learn to die,' you 'prepare' for the last extremity; but there is the last quarter of an hour (or the last second), and at that point it is death that completes the last leg of the journey by itself, and is a surprise. In this sense, it is not a possibility like all the other possibilities, in which there is always a preliminary, always a project. To be 'unassumable' belongs to its very quality. It is an event without project. The 'project' one may have of death is undone at the last moment. It is death alone that goes the last leg. Not us. We do not, strictly speaking, meet it.

Spinoza will say, as you know, that philosophers should think of nothing less than of death. Heidegger, by contrast, is the one who pursued philosophical thought's reference to death the farthest. The philosopher's mortality marks his thought as it does his existence. A finite existence. A finite human existence, even if philosophical. Philosophical thought because of that finitude. Heidegger calls the extreme possibility of death possibility of impossibility. Without wishing to play on words, I have always thought that possibility implied a human power, whereas dying is 'unassumable': it is rather 'an impossibility of possibility.'

155

That which is inevitable, and yet for us, in the strict sense of the term, impossible?

The inexorable, in the sense in which I said just a moment ago. From that point of view, it is resistant to knowledge, in an exceptional way. It is not at all the unknown because consciousness is limited in fact but could someday miraculously expand. Death can never be known. It is in this sense that I said a moment ago that the 'unassumable' belongs to its quality. Those who return from the last extremity and tell about it have not been there. It's not serious.

The world of the Cave remains closed upon itself and its shadows, and we are none the wiser about it today, according to you, than is Book Ten of Plato's Republic, *nor than our great-grandchildren will be, about this essential point of human fate? Is death the Sphinx we question but that does not answer?*

Yes. And the word mystery is appropriate here. It is the locus of that category: the mystery. An unknown that raises a question. A question without givens. It does not involve the tireless emphasis of the self-evident banality that we don't know what lies beyond death. We don't even know what meaning the *beyond* might have in this circumstance. Even the famous nothingness people agree about so readily is problematic. Can one break with being? Can one *exit* being? Don't negation and annihilation leave in place the stage on which negations and annihilations are played out? Isn't the outside inside, in a sense? Aren't we always enclosed within existence? No escape.

Maurice Blanchot, in his wonderful and strange work, has conceived of death in terms of the impossibility of breaking away. This view on the mystery of death is profound and obsessive. Ontology as obsession. In the anguish of death, the impossibility of nothingness. An impossibility of 'stopping the music' or of calling a halt to the 'ruckus' of existence! And yet, at the same time, the impossibility of going on with them.

But along those same lines couldn't we also say, on the positive side, that nothing entirely new comes along in our existence except death? It is the intrusion of the unknown, the never heretofore, in a world in which everything will soon have happened. The mystery of death is also the possibility of something different. At least some would say so.

We'll talk about that other aspect of death. Something new does in fact take place; but for us who witness the death of the other person; we'll never know what it means to the deceased himself. We don't even know what legitimacy there may be in the expression, 'to the deceased himself.' But for the survivor, there is in the death of the other his or her disappearance, and the extreme loneliness of that disappearance. I think that *the Human* consists precisely in opening oneself to the death of the other, in being preoccupied with his or her death. What I am saying here may seem like a pious thought, but I am persuaded that around the death of my neighbour what I have been calling the humanity of man is manifested.

To receive into one's thought and one's heart the perspective of the death of the other is surely an act of piety – but also of thought?

Yes.

Gabriel Marcel said that to love is 'to tell the other, "You won't die, not you"'. Which is to recognize, thanks to the look of love, that the other's death is impossible, and at the same time the impossible of death. In this sense, can one say that death arrests the project of being? It continues otherwise, but continues nonetheless, and not just in our memory and thought. Can we not reintegrate even the death of the other into a new project?

Gabriel Marcel believes in the metaphysical efficacy of love, and does not think the excluded middle is thinkable.

Plato has Socrates say that he accepts running 'the noble risk of immortality.' Isn't that a kind of continuity of the project, across the hiatus? One changes plans, and even lives, but one who was only mortal sees the possibility, the eventuality, open up, of becoming immortal by passing through death. To run this risk but also to take up this hope – is this not precisely what is human, terribly human?

Alexander Kojève liked to remind us, on the subject of that moment when Socrates was about to convince his interlocutors of the immortality of the soul, and they were half hoping to see Socrates after his death and half in despair before the imminent separation, that Plato himself was not present at the conversation and consequently did not share the emotion of those interlocutors. Did he not note, at the beginning of the dialogue, that he had been absent due to sickness? We will never know, therefore, whether he was convinced on the point of immortality by the proofs in the *Phaedo*; or whether he had run the noble risk of believing in it. . . . If we are to believe Kojève, at least, in whom there is no lack of ingenious and penetrating ideas.

But is it not the case that a philosopher's reflection can and must extend that far, i.e. to the point of risking the unknown, of embracing that 'noble risk of immortality' that death makes us run? It that not to take into account what is most human in thought?

In my opinion that alternative of being and nothingness on which the proof of immortality is based fails to pose the primary question. *To be or not to be* is not the ultimate alternative, and in any case not the

159

ultimate or most urgent question. We'll come back to this point. It is true, of course, that to speak of questions of life and death is to speak of urgent questions. But is the couple life and death reducible to being and not being? Is it not a metaphor for it? We must get back to the concrete consideration of death.

The couple is, concretely, indissociable. Life cannot be thought of as if death did not exist, but conversely, human life, precisely insofar as it is human, raises questions about human death, which is not the death of just anything. Of what is it the death, exactly? Is it the death of love, which is doubtless more than being? To love or not to love is assuredly the more profound form of the question: To be or not to be? We know that death is an end, but we don't know of what, nor do we know whether it is not also a beginning.

When death is there, we are no longer there. Is it an end or a beginning? Let's concede that we know nothing about it. Perhaps we don't yet realize to what extent all that is unknown. The idea of the excluded middle stakes out the unknown and mysterious domain of the question of death. Just now I alluded to the death-life metaphor. We use those two words constantly as we live our daily lives, carried along by our perseverance in being, forgetful of our properly human vocation of disinterestedness, i.e. of disengagement with respect to our being and care for the being of the other. Moreover, I always try to introduce the idea that mystery is ineluctable in the description and terminology of death. We must consider the other face of that violence that unfolds in death, precisely because it is not assumable; not by anyone. But before the death of the other, my neighbour, death the mysterious appears to me, in any case, as the bringing about of an aloneness toward which I cannot be indifferent. It awakens me to the other.

Heidegger deduces all conceivable meaning from the attitude of man toward his own death. He thinks to the very end, in the senses of the term. He carries out his thought to its ultimate consequences, and he thinks that my death for me can be nothing but the ultimate self. I wonder if that is, in fact, for thought, the ultimate movement to the end. Is there not a manner of thinking that goes beyond my own death to the death of the other man, and does not the human consist precisely in this thinking beyond one's own death? I have no desire to exhibit some noble soul in affirming this. What I mean is, the death of the other can constitute a central experience for me, whatever the resources of our perseverance in our own being may be. For me, for example (and this will hardly surprise you) the Holocaust is an event of still inexhaustible meaning. But in any death to which we are present, and I would even say in any approach to a mortal man, the reverberations of that extraordinary unknown can be heard. We apprehend it irresistibly in the encounter with death in the other man.

The significance of that event is infinite, its emotion ethical through and through.

The death of the other whom we love confers upon death all its dramatic intensity, because the life of the other has beamed forth all its intensity. It is not only the death of the other; it seems the death of love, in which the other took on for us the fullness of his being and life, and an identity irreducible to any other. It is impossible for it to pass unnoticed, that it be hidden; and when death touches the loved other, it touches our common love: it is our own death that is announced to us. When we lose one of our own, as the saying goes, we enter into intimate relations with death; its presence becomes more familiar, and we discover how much it is interwoven into our lives.

It is not the intensity that I have in mind, and my analysis does not set out from a relation to the death of those 'dear to us,' and has even less affinity with a return to 'oneself,' which would take us back to the priority of my own death. In speaking of the Holocaust, I am thinking of the death of the other man. I am thinking of the other man, for whom, I know not why, one can feel oneself to be already a responsible survivor. I have asked myself (perhaps you know this) what the face of the other man means. I have allowed myself to say that there is in him in the first instance a directness and a rectitude: a being-face-to-face, precisely as if he were exposed to some threat at point blank range, as if he were about to be delivered to his death. I have sometimes wondered whether the idea of the straight line – that shortest distance between two points – is not originally the line according to which the face I encounter is exposed to death. That is probably the way my death stares me in the face, but I do not see my own death. The first obvious thing in the other's face is the directness of exposure and that defenselessness. The human being in his face is the most naked; nakedness itself. But at the same time, his face faces. It is in his way of being all alone in his facing that the violence of death is to be assessed.

A third moment in the epiphany of the face: it requires me. The face looks at me, calls out to me. It claims me. What does it ask for? Not to leave it alone. An answer: Here I am. My presence, of no avail perhaps, but a gratuitous movement of presence and responsibility for the other. To answer, Here I am, is already the encounter with the face.

In truth, its very singularity only appears at a moment that extreme, that ultimate. We often say that she or he looks like so-and-so. In that instant, it is clear that he doesn't look like anyone but himself – that person one loved, or didn't love – and no one else can take his place.

If we want to define what that famous love of one's neighbour – a shop-worn saying – is, I think we have to return to that relation to the face qua mortality of one's neighbour and the impossibility of leaving him to his isolation. The positive definition of the love of one's neighbour is to be distinguished from all that is erotic and concupiscence. Love without concupiscence; it is sociality itself. In that relation with the face, in a direct relation with the death of the other, you probably discover that the death of the other has priority over yours, and over your life. I am not merely speaking of the 'banal' fact that one can die for another. That banal fact that is not at all banal or simple is the foray of the human, putting in question the ontological necessities and the persistence of being persevering in its being. Without knowing how to swim, to jump into the water to save someone is to go toward the other totally, without holding back anything of oneself. To give oneself totally to the other to respond to his unspoken request, to the expression of his face, to his mortality, his 'Thou shalt not kill.' But above all, it is no longer just a question of going toward the other when he is dying, but of answering with one's presence the mortality of the living. That is the whole of ethical conduct. In the final analysis, the ultimate scruple is to not push the other back into some third – or fourth – world by the place in the sun I myself occupy. Pascal said: 'My place in the sun is the archetype and the beginning of the usurpation of the whole world.' As if, by the fact of being there, I were depriving someone of his living space, as if I were expelling or murdering someone. It was also Pascal who said: 'The *I* is hateful.' He was not merely giving us a lesson in good manners or style, but of ontology. As is the principle of identity positing itself triumphantly as *I* carried with it an indecency and violence, as if the *I* prohibited, by its very positing, the full existence of the other; as if in appropriating something it ran the risk of depriving someone else of something.

Simone Weil also said: 'I look at the world as if I were not in it.' Could it be that that supreme form of detachment and of contemplation, which is the opposite of indifference, seeks perhaps in the world and in man the original and infinite purity that they contain? It is an attempt to deliver the world from the opaqueness of our presence, from the obstacle constituted by our presence between a pure look and its true object. Is it not in the same way that Racine's Phèdre ends up, guilty and ashamed of being so? 'And death, robbing my eyes of their light, restores to the day the purity they sullied.'

I think those quotes concur on many points with what I was trying to suggest. Behind the relation with the death of the other, a very strange problem is raised. Is our desire-to-be legitimate on the part of us humans, even at the level of being? It is not a question of asking ourselves in the name of I know not what abstract law whether we shouldn't take our own lives, but of finding reasons to live, to be worthy of being. The bad conscience of being, coming to light when confronted with the death of the other! Is

165

it not a hearkening to the commandment to love that the face of mortals transmits to us? Of their right to be there can be no doubt, but it is the *I* that is the singular locus in which the problem arises. The effort to exist, the aspiration to persevere in being, the *conatus essendi* is, according to philosophers like Spinoza, the beginning of all rights. That is precisely what I try to put in question on the basis of the encounter with mortality – or the face – of the other, insisting, obviously, on the radical difference between the *others* and *me*. The anguish for my own death reveals my *finitude* and the scandal of an existence dying always too soon. The good conscience of being remains intact in that finitude. It is the death of the other that challenges that good conscience.

All others do not, however, exist equally for us. They exist more or less, and their death exists more or less, according to whether their presence resonates closer or more remotely in our lives. For all kinds of reasons. But when we have seen death touch the face of a being we love, it can happen that it appears to us at once more horrible and easier, desirable almost. It is life that becomes foreign, and we almost seem to pass from the horror of dying to that of living, of surviving the beloved. Death takes on, after a fashion, the traits of that beloved face, and through it becomes attractive, and instead of frightening us, familiar. In short, to share such a fate becomes enviable in the name of love. And in that name only. All the great lovers of history wish to follow the other to the tomb, and sometimes do so. They make light of life and death. Do we perhaps shed our I in a death that truly touches us?

Death, in that case, has lost its sting.

It gives rise, as it were, to the other's call, a call of love. In any case, it presents itself as a deliverance. It saves us from living a half life.

But that is not an ethical attitude. On the contrary, I was speaking of the ethical attitude that is at the basis of sociality. Not of the attitude toward the death of a being already chosen and dear, but of the death of the first-one-to-come-along. To perceive that we come after an other whoever he may be – that is ethics.

It is a kind of break with an ontology in which our own being conditions the approach of Being and of beings. All that counts, after all, is the existence of the other, and therefore the death of the other?

It is on the basis of the existence of the other that my own existence is posited as human. I try to imagine an anthropology – a bit different from the one taking its cue from the *conatus essendi* – setting out from the relation to the death of the other. But I believe I said that we are answerable not only for the death of the other but for his life as well. And it is in being answerable for his life that we are already with him in his death. As for ontology, I have sometimes wondered whether, in order to reveal the human that strives to break free, it should be grounded or undermined.

12

Violence of the Face

The global significance of your work is to find the meaning of being beyond being – to relativize history and the system by that which does not belong to the system: the face of the other, which is in the trace of the Infinite. Is that key to the reading of your work correct?

I wouldn't say the *meaning of being*, but *meaning*: a rationality, an intelligibility. The important idea, when I speak of the face of the other, the trace of Infinity, or the Word of God, is that of a signifying of meaning that, originally, is not a theme, is not an object of any field of knowledge, is not the being of a being, is not representation. A God that concerns me by a Word [*Parole*] expressed in the guise of the face of the other man is a transcendence that never becomes immanence. The face of the other is his way of signifying. I also use another formula: God never takes on a body. He never becomes, in the proper sense of the word, a being. That is his invisibility. That idea is essential in the reading of my book: *De Dieu qui vient à l'idée* [*Of God who comes to mind*].

Why doesn't the face that I encounter in everyday life

belong to history, why is it not a phenomenon, a simple experience? Why does it tear itself free from context?

I have always described the face of the neighbour as the bearer of an order, imposing upon me, with respect to the other, a gratuitous and non-transferable responsibility, as if the *I* were chosen and unique – and in which the other were absolutely other, i.e., still incomparable, and thus unique. But the men round about me are multiple. Hence the question: 'Who is my neighbour?' The inevitable question of justice. The necessity of comparing incomparables, of knowing men; hence their appearance as plastic forms of faces that are visible and, one might say, 'de-faced' [*dé-visagés*]: like a grouping from which the uniqueness of the face is torn free, as from a context, the source of my obligation toward other men; the source to which the quest for justice goes back, in the final analysis, and the forgetfulness of which risks transforming the sublime and difficult work of justice into a purely political calculation – to the point of totalitarian abuse.

Historicism, materialism, structuralism, ontology: would the limit of all these philosophical figures be their fundamental inability to go beyond being and history, their restriction of meaning to being?

By and large that is so. But I am not tempted by a philosophy of history and I am not certain of its finality. I don't say that all is for the best, and the idea of progress doesn't seem to me very reliable. But I think that responsibility for the other man, or, if you like, the epiphany of the human face, constitutes a penetration of the crust, so to speak, of 'being persevering in its being' and preoccupied with itself. Responsibility for the other, the 'dis-interested' for-the-other of saintliness. I'm not saying men are saints, or moving toward saintliness. I'm only saying that the vocation of saintliness is recognized by all human beings as a value, and that this recognition defines the human. The human has pierced through imperturbable being; even if no social organization, nor any institution can, in the name of purely ontological necessities, ensure, or even produce saintliness. There have been saints.

Then we must read the nihilist outcome of contemporary philosophy not as a destiny of philosophy as such, but only as the result of that philosophy which, as ontology, does not accept the risk of the beyond being of transcendence?

Very well, but I would add that my propositions do not pretend to the exclusivism of the philosophers of history. If, in my view, the very origin of intelligibility and meaning go back to responsibility for the other man, the fact of the matter is that ontology, objective knowledge and political forms are commanded by this meaning or are necessary to its

171

signifying. I said earlier that the origin of the meaningful in the face of the other, confronted with the
actual plurality of human beings – calls for justice
and knowledge; the exercise of justice demands courts
of law and political institutions, and even, paradoxically, a certain violence that is implied in all justice.
Violence is originally justified as the defense of the
other, of the *neighbour* (be he a relation of mine, or
my people!), but is violence for someone.

*The notion of meaning is fundamental in your work.
In the more recent writings, it reappears continually.
What is the philosophical status of that notion? Is it
really certain that philosophy must seek meaning?*

Except that the philosopher and the scholar who
reason and judge and the statesman will not be
excluded from the spiritual. But its meaning is originally in the human, in the initial fact that man is
concerned with the other man. It is at the basis of the
banality according to which few things interest man
as much as does the other man.

I cannot further explain this moment in which, in
the weight of being, rationality begins. A first notion
of signifying, to which reason may be traced, and that
cannot be reduced to anything else. It is phenomeno-
logically irreducible: meaning means.

To seek the definition of meaning is as if one were
to try reduce the effect of a poem to its causes or
transcendental conditions. The definition of poetry is

perhaps that the poetic vision is more true and, in a certain sense 'older' than the vision of its conditions. In reflecting on the transcendental conditions of the poem, you have already lost the poem.

You reject the perspective of the indefinite dissemination of meaning. Would it be accurate to say that your conclusions are the opposite of those of the theoreticians of writing [écriture], Derrida and Blanchot?

Yes and no, because I have great esteem for both of them and I admire their speculative gifts. On many points I concur with their analyses. But it isn't in terms of writing [*écriture*] that problems come to me, and with respect to Writ [*Ecriture*] – the Holy – perhaps our positions diverge. I have often wondered, with respect to Derrida, whether the *différance* of the present which leads him to the deconstruction of notions does not attest to the prestige that eternity retains in his eyes, the 'great present,' *being*, which corresponds to the priority of the *theoretical* and the truth of the theoretical, in relation to which temporality would be failure. I wonder if time – in its very dia-chrony – isn't *better* than eternity and the order of the Good itself.

Dia-chrony – beyond the syn-chrony of all eternal presentness – is it not the nodal point of the irreversible (or dis-inter-ested) relation of the *I* to the neighbour that, precisely from me to the other, is impossible synchrony and yet at the same time non-

173

in-difference and, like a farewell [*à-Dieu*], already love?

Is it really possible to exclude all analogical mediation in the use of human language about God?

I don't exclude that language in the least, but perhaps I insist on not forgetting its metaphorical meaning. But what I am looking for is what Husserl calls *Originäre Gegebenheit*: the 'concrete circumstances' in which a meaning comes to mind in the first place. It is not a gratuitous or vain quest for some kind of chronological priority. I think the most productive thing phenomenology has contributed is the insistence on the fact that the look absorbed by the datum has already *forgotten* to relate it to the entirety of the mental procedure that conditions the upsurge of the datum, and thus to its concrete meaning. The datum – separated from the all that has been forgotten – is but an *abstraction*, whose '*mise-en-scène*' is reconstructed by phenomenology. Husserl always speaks of the 'blinders' that deform naïve vision. It is not just a question of the narrowness of its objective field, but of the obnubilation of its psychic horizons; as if the naïvely given object already veiled the eyes that seize it. To see philosophically, i.e., without naïve blindness, is to reconstitute for the naïve look (which is still that of positive science) the concrete situation of appearing; it is to carry out its phenomenology, to return to the neglected concrete-

ness of its *'mise-en-scène'* that offers up the *meaning* of
the datum, and, behind its *quiddity*, its mode of being.

To seek the 'origin' of the word God, the concrete
circumstances of its signifying, is absolutely necessary.
One begins by accepting his Word in the name of the
social authority of religion. How to be sure that the
Word thus accepted is indeed that spoken by God?
The original experience must be sought. Philosophy
– or phenomenology – is necessary to recognize His
voice. I have thought that it is in the face of the other
that he speaks to me for 'the first time.' It is in the
encounter with the other man that he 'comes to my
mind' or 'falls beneath the sense' [*tombe sous le sens*].

*One has the impression that in a sense you wanted to
reverse the relation of exclusion between reason and
violence proposed by Eric Weil, in affirming, to the
contrary, the close solidarity of the two within totalitarian
discourse.*

I have great admiration for the work, and much
piety for the memory, of Eric Weil. At no time have
I tried to exclude justice – that would be stupid –
from the human order. But I have made an attempt
to return to justice from what one might call charity,
and which appears to me as an unlimited obligation
toward the other, and in this sense accession to his
uniqueness as a person, and in this sense love: disinterested love, without concupiscence. I have already told
you how that initial obligation, before the multiplicity

of human beings, becomes justice. But it is very important, in my view, that justice should flow from, issue from, the preeminence of the other. The institutions that justice requires must be subject to the oversight of the charity from which justice issued. Justice, inseparable from institutions, and hence from politics, risks preventing the face of the other man from being recognized. The pure rationality of justice in Eric Weil, as in Hegel, succeeds in making us conceive of the particularity of the human being as negligible and as if it were not that of a uniqueness, but of an anonymous individuality. The determinism of the rational totality runs the risk of totalitarianism, which doesn't, in fact, abandon ethical language and has always spoken – and still speaks of *the good* and *the best*, the famous language of 'proud things' of *Psalms* 12:4.[1] Fascism itself never glorified crime. Therefore I say that E. Weil, a philosopher and an infinitely respectable man, has had thoughts more utopian than mine, precisely because it is very difficult to ensure oneself against totalitarianism by a politics of the pure concept that taxes the attachment to the *uniqueness* of the other and the radical *for-the-other* of the *I* with subjectivism. It seems to me that rational justice is compromised when the relation with the other is visibly profaned. And there, between purely rational justice and injustice, there is an appeal to the 'wisdom' of the *I*, the possibilities of which perhaps don't include any principle that can be formulated *a priori*.

176

Violence of the Face

You affirm that your way of naming God belongs strictly to philosophical discourse, and not to religion. To religion would belong the task of consolation, not of demonstration. What does that mean, exactly? Is religion perhaps something superfluous?

The question is more complex. Both moments are necessary; they are not on the same level. What I want to show is the transcendence in natural thought in the approach to the other. Natural theology is necessary in order subsequently to recognize the voice and 'accent' of God in the Scriptures themselves. A necessity that is perhaps the motivating force behind religious philosophy itself. The seducer knows all the ploys of language and all its ambiguities. He knows all the terms of the dialectic. He exists precisely as a moment of human freedom, and the most dangerous of seducers is the one who carries you away with pious words to violence and contempt for the other man.

What is the correct position of the relationship between Judaism and Hellenism that you propose?

I'm in favor of the Greek heritage. It is not at the beginning, but everything must be able to be 'translated' into Greek. The translation of the Scriptures by the Septuagintal scholars symbolizes that necessity. It's the theme of a text from the Talmud, that I had occasion to do a commentary on last year. There is, as you know, a legend about the translation of the Bible into Greek. Ptolemy is said to have chosen seventy Jewish scholars and locked them up in separate rooms to translate the Jewish Bible into Greek. Supposedly they all translated it the same way, and even the corrections they felt obliged to make to the text were the same. Father Barthélemy, a professor at the Catholic University of Fribourg, has said: 'It is obviously the fanciful idea of a guide made up for the tourists visiting the place.' In the Talmud, that story is gone over. It is clearly, for rabbinic thought, an apologue, a midrash. The Talmud wanted to approve both the translation of the Bible into Greek and the principle of correction. There are ideas that have their original meaning in biblical thought and that must be related differently in Greek. But Greek is a language of impartial thought, of the universality of pure knowledge. All meaning, all intelligibility, all spirit is not knowledge, but all can be translated into Greek. With periphrases it is possible to give an account of a spirituality resistant to the forms of knowledge.

What I call Greek is the way of our university language, which we inherited from the Greeks. At the university, even at Catholic and Hebrew universities, we speak Greek even when and if we don't know an alpha from an omega.

The transformation of ontological categories into ethical ones proceeds to the point of putting the new

*fundamental question: 'Do I have the right to be?'
Does that question belong to the consciousness of original
sin?*

I think that philosophical discourse is independent
of that guilt, and that the question, 'Do I have the
right to be?' expresses primarily the human in its care
for the other. I have written a lot on this theme; it's
my main theme now. My place in being, the *Da-* of
my *Dasein* [the there of my being-there] – isn't it
already usurpation, already violence with respect to
the other? A preoccupation that has nothing ethereal,
nothing abstract about it. The press speaks to us of
the Third World, and we are quite comfortable here;
we're sure of our daily meals. At whose cost, we may
wonder.

Pascal said: the *I* is hateful. In the sovereign
affirmation of the *I*, the perseverance of beings in
their being is repeated, but also consciousness of the
horror that egotism arouses in this myself. Pascal also
says that my place in the sun is the archetype and the
beginning of the usurpation of the whole earth.

One can't say that Pascal didn't know about original sin, but I wonder whether the human as such is
not sufficient for this supreme scruple – whether
scruples are always already remorse.

*Somebody wrote that the ethical responsibility you
speak of is abstract and devoid of concrete content. Does
that seem a valid critique to you?*

I have never claimed to describe human reality in its immediate appearance, but what human depravation itself cannot obliterate: the human vocation to saintliness. I don't affirm human saintliness; I say that man cannot question the supreme value of saintliness. In 1968, the year of questioning in and around the universities, all values were 'up for grabs,' with the exception of the value of the 'other man,' to which one was to dedicate oneself. The young people who for hours abandoned themselves to all sorts of fun and unruliness went at the end of the day to visit the 'striking Renault workers' as if to pray. Man is the being who recognizes saintliness and the forgetting of self. The 'for oneself' is always open to suspicion. We live in a state in which the idea of justice is superimposed on that initial charity, but it is in that initial charity that the human resides; justice itself can be traced back to it. Man is not only the being who understands what being means, as Heidegger would have it, but the being who has already heard and understood the commandment of saintliness in the face of the other man. Even when it is said that at the origin there are altruistic instincts, there is the recognition that God has already spoken. He began to speak very early. The anthropological meaning of instinct! In the daily Jewish liturgy, the first morning prayer says: 'Blessed art thou, O Lord, our God, King of the Universe, who giveth the cock knowledge to distinguish between day and night.' In the crowing of the cock, the first Revelation: the awakening to the light.

Does peace have a future? What is Christianity's contribution to its construction?

Oh, you're asking me for a prophesy! It is true that all men are prophets. Doesn't Moses say (*Numbers* 11:29): 'Would that all the Lord's people were prophets,' and doesn't Amos go further – all humanity: 'The Lord God hath spoken, Who can but prophesy?' (*Amos* 3:8). And yet it is difficult for me to make predictions – unless the verses I just quoted are themselves favorable prophesies.

I also think the trials humanity has passed through in the course of the twentieth century are, in their horror, not only a measure of human depravity, but a renewed call back to our vocation. I have the impression they have altered something in us. I think specifically that the Passion of Israel at Auschwitz has profoundly marked Christianity itself and that a Judeo-Christian friendship is an element of peace, in which the person of Jean-Paul II represents hope.

What is the value of liturgy and prayer?

One doesn't pray for oneself. Nevertheless, the Jewish prayer, the daily prayer, replaces the sacrifices of the Temple, according to Jewish theology. But then, like the sacrifice of the Temple which was a holocaust, it is in its entirety an offering. There is an exception when one prays for Israel persecuted. In that case one prays for the community, but it is a

181

prayer for the people called to reveal the glory of God. In praying to God, it is still for God that one is praying in this case as well.

When you are truly in distress, you can mention it in prayer. But are you going to eliminate in this manner a suffering that wipes away sins in expiating them? If you want to escape your own suffering, how will you expiate your wrong-doings? The question is more complex. <u>In our suffering God suffers with us.</u> Doesn't the Psalmist say (*Psalms* 91:15): 'I am with him in distress'? It is God who suffers most in human suffering. The *I* who suffers prays for the suffering of God, who suffers by the sin of man and the painful expiation for sin. A kenosis of God! Prayer, altogether, is not for oneself.

There aren't many souls who pray with that prayer of the just. Surely there are many levels. I have presented you with the most rigorous of theological conceptions. Perhaps it is important to know it. I think the less elevated forms of prayer retain much of its piety.

Bibliographical Note

Philosophy and Transcendence was first published as 'Philosophie et transcendance' in the *Encyclopédie philosophique universelle*, (Presses Universitaires de France, 1989).

Totality and Totalization and *Infinity* was originally published as 'Totalité et totalisation' and 'Infini' in the *Encyclopaedia Universalis*, Paris: Encyclopedia Universalis (Paris, 1968).

Beyond Dialogue was first published as 'Par delà le dialogue' in the *Journal des communautés*, (Paris: Consistoire Israëlite, 1967.

The Word I, the Word You, and the Word God was first published as 'Le mot je, le mot toi, le mot Dieu' in *Le Monde*, 1978.

The Proximity of the Other was first published as 'La proximité de l'autre,' a conversation with Anne-Catherine Benchelah, in *Phréatique*, 1986.

Utopia and Socialism was originally published as the preface to Martin Buber's *Utopie et Socialisme*, Aubier-Montaigne, 1977.

The Prohibition against Representation and 'The Rights of Man' was first published as 'Interdit de la représentation et "Droits de l'homme"', *Interdit de la représentation – Colloque de Montpellier, Seuil*, 1981.

183

Peace and Proximity was originally published as 'Paix et proximité' in *Les Cahiers de la nuit surveillée*, No. 3, (Paris: Verdier, 1984).

The Rights of the Other Man was first published as 'Les droits de l'autre homme' in *Les droits de l'homme en question*, La documentation française, 1989.

The Philosopher and Death was originally published as 'Le philosophe et la mort,' an interview with Christian Chabanis, 'La mort, un terme ou un commencement?', Fayard, 1982.

Violence of the Face was originally published as 'Violence du visage,' an interview with Angelo Bianchi, in *Hermeneutica*, 1985.

Notes

Foreword

1. L'Herne, no. 60 (1991): 76–7
2. Idem., p. 80.
3. Idem., pp. 81–2.
4. Wahl, *Traité de Métaphysique* (Paris: Payot, 1953), p. 721. Quoted in E. Levinas, *Outside the Subject* (London: The Athlone Press, 1993), p. 82.
5. E. Levinas, *Totality and Infinity* (Pittsburgh: Duquesne University Press, n.d. [1969]), p. 274.
6. E. Levinas, 'Philosophy and the Idea of Infinity,' Collected Philosophical Papers, edited and translated by A. Lingis (Dordrecht: Martinus Nijhoff, 1987), p. 54.
7. L'Herne, no. 60, (1991): 81.
8. J.-P. Sartre, *Being and Nothingness* (New York: Simon & Schuster, 1966).
9. [This work, which is a translation from Hebrew of Martin Buber's *Netivot be-utopyah*, is available in English as *Paths in Utopia* (New York: Macmillan, 1950) It appears as chapter 3 of the present volume. – Trans.]
10. See also E. Levinas, *De Dieu qui vient à l'idée* (Paris: J. Vrin, 1986), pp. 211–30.

11. See also *Proper Names* (London: The Athlone Press, 1996), pp. 17–39, and *Outside the Subject* (London: The Athlone Press, 1993), pp. 4–48.

12. See also *Outside the Subject*, pp. 116–25, and *Entre nous* (London: The Athlone Press, 1998), pp. 155–8.

13. *Totality and Infinity*, p. 213. [Translation slightly altered. – Trans.] See also *Otherwise than Being or Beyond Essence* (The Hague: Martinus Nijhoff, 1981), p. 158.

14. *Totality and Infinity*, p. 295. [Translation slightly altered. – Trans.]

Chapter 1: Philosophy and Transcendence

1. Levinas, *De Dieu qui vient à l'idée* (Paris: J. Vrin, [1982]1986), p. 163. [Excerpted from a piece titled 'Herméneutique et au-delà,' available in English as 'Hermeneutics and the Beyond,' *Entre nous* (London: The Athlone Press, 1998), pp. 65–75. Translation slightly altered. – Trans.]

2. *Enneades*, Tractate 5, chap. 3, para. 11. [In order to remain as close as possible to Levinas's interpretation, I translate his French version of the text, but for purposes of comparison I append the translation of S. MacKenna and B. S. Page, published in the Great Books of the Western World Series, No. 17: *Plotinus: The Six Enneads* (Chicago: Encyclopaedia Britannica, Inc., 1952), p. 222. – Trans.] 'It knows the Transcendent in very essence but, with all its effort to grasp that prior as a pure unity, it goes forth amassing successive impressions, so that, to it, the object becomes multi-

ple. . . . If it had not possessed a previous impression of the Transcendent, it could never have grasped it, but this impression, originally of unity, has become an impression of multiplicity, and the Intellect-Principle, in taking cognizance of that multiplicity, knows the Transcendent and so is realized as an eye possessed of its vision.'

3. *Enneades*, Tractate 5, chap. 1, para. 6.
4. *Enneades*, Tractate 5, chap. 1, para. 4.
5. [*The Crisis of European Sciences and Transcendental Phenomenology* (Evanston: Northwestern University Press, 1970). – Trans.]
6. [Loosely quoted from Corneille's *Cinna*, Act 5, Scene 3, in which Auguste declares: 'Je suis maître de moi comme de l'Univers.' – Trans.]
7. [Pascal's *Pensées*, in *Pascal* (Chicago: Encyclopaedia Britannica, Inc., Great Books of the Western World Series, no. 33, 1952), p. 226. – Trans.]
8. [Clearly the sense of utopia intended here is the etymological one: 'no place.' – Trans.]
9. [The article 'Philosophie et transcendence' from the *Encyclopédie philosophique universelle*, Presses Universitaires de France, 1989, which appears to be the earliest version of this text (as well as all subsequent versions) has: 'Cette façon de me réclamer, de me mettre en cause et d'en appeler à moi, à ma responsabilité pour la mort d'autrui, est une signification à tel point irréductible, que c'est à partir d'elle que le sens de la mort doit être entendu, par delà la dialectique abstraite de l'être et de sa négation à

laquelle, à partir de la violence ramenée à la négation et à l'anéantissement, on dit la mort.' I have assumed that the word 'dit' should be 'réduit,' based on grammatical considerations as well as my interpretation of the overall meaning of the passage. – Trans.]

10. [Levinas uses the term concretization (*concrétude*), in opposition to abstraction, in a way that suggests the same phenomenological approach he designates elsewhere as deformalization (*déformalisation*). It appears to have the same sense as 'concrétisation' in *Totalité et infini* (The Hague: Martinus Nijhoff, 1961), p. 21; *Totality and Infinity* (Pittsburgh: Duquesne University Press, n.d. [1969]), p. 50, where its meaning is closely connected with 'deformalization'. – Trans.]

11. [Levinas uses the word *'signifier,'* which can mean both to signify or to order (to issue a command). There seems to be a blending of both meanings in the present context, which would not be out of keeping with Levinas's tendency toward ethical heteronomy. – Trans.]

12. [Levinas uses the French term *'s'effrayer,'* a reflexive verb, and emphasizes the reflexivity by italicizing the elided reflexive pronoun 'se.' The ensuing analysis turns upon Heidegger's notion that the reflexives denote a return to an auto-affectivity of 'Befindlichkeit,' rejected by Levinas because it suggests a return to the self, or perhaps a failure to leave it. – Trans.]

Notes

Chapter 3: Infinity

1. Descartes, *Meditations*, III [Descartes, *Discourse on Method and The Meditations* (London and New York: Penguin Classics, 1968), p. 126.
2. [See Plato's *The Sophist*, 241d. Levinas alludes to the same 'parricide' in *Proper Names* (Stanford: Stanford University Press, 1996), p. 61, and *Humanism de l'autre homme* (Montpellier: Fata Morgana, Livre de Poche, [1972] 1987), p. 10. – Trans.]
3. [*Allgemeine Naturgeschichte und Theorie des Himmels* (Königsberg and Leipzig, 1755). English translation by W. Hastie in *Kant's Cosmogony* (Glasgow, 1900), reprinted as *Kant's Cosmogony: As in His Essay on Retardation of the Rotation of the Earth* (Greenwood: Greenwood Press, 1969). – Trans.]

Chapter 4: Beyond Dialogue

1. Edmond Fleg, *Jesus: told by the Wandering Jew* (New York: E .P. Dutton, 1935).

Chapter 5: The Word I, the Word You, the Word God

1. [For further comments on the affinities between Buber and Marcel, see 'Martin Buber, Gabriel Marcel and Philosophy,' *Outside the Subject* (London: The Athlone Press, 1994), pp. 20–39. – Trans.]
2. Pascal, *Pensées* (Pensée No. 479), tr. W. F. Trotter in *Great Books of the Western World*, ed. Mortimer J. Adler, vol. 30 (Chicago: University of Chicago Press, 1990), p. 257.

Chapter 6: The Proximity of the Other

1. [The French is 'qui n'est pas à venir, mais qui advient.' I have interpreted the difference between 'venir' and 'advenir' as one in which the latter term conveys an 'adventitiousness' or unforeseen element, rather than just the futurity of the 'à venir.' – Trans.]

2. [The material paraphrased and quoted here is taken from Vasily Grossman's *Life and Fate* (New York: Harper Row, 1985), pp. 404–11. Translation slightly altered. – Trans.]

Chapter 8: The Prohibition against Representation and 'The Right of Man'

1. It suffices on this subject to consult the treatises Rosh-Hashannah (p. 24a) and Avodah Zarah (p. 42b–43a) of the Babylonian Talmud.

2. See the treatises Rosh-Hashannah (p. 24b) and Avodah Zarah (p. 43a).

3. See my study, 'Reality and its shadow,' reprinted in *Les imprévus de l'histoire*, Fata Morgana, 1994.

4. See esp. section 27 of *Ideen I*, p. 50.

5. See my study, 'Lévy-Bruhl et la philosophie contemporaine,' in *Revue philosophique de la France et de l'étranger*, no. 4, 1957, esp. pp. 558–61: 'La ruine de la représentation.' [This piece can be found in English in Levinas's *Entre Nous: Essays on Thinking-of-the-Other* (London: The Athlone Press, 1998), chap. 3. – Trans.]

Notes

Chapter 9: Peace and Proximity
1. Verse 7 in Christian bibles.

Chapter 12: Violence and the Face
1. [Verse 3 in Christian bibles. Levinas uses the term 'grandes phrases,' the term used in the *Bible de Jérusalem* – Trans.]

Index

Index

Index

morality, 91
Moses, 181
murder, 23, 28
nakedness, 24, 33
natura naturans, 68

Nazism, 83
Newton, 66
Nicholas of Cusa, 65, 66
Nietzsche, 55
non-indifference, 93, 94, 173, 174
Numbers 11:29, 181

Origen, 63

Parmenides, 6, 61
parricide, 61
Pascal, 21–3, 61, 66, 95, 179
perception, 3, 14, 16, 17, 40, 42, 43
Plato, 31, 47, 50, 59, 61, 64
Plotinus, 7, 8, 9, 50, 62
poetry, 172
presence, 4, 6, 11, 13, 14, 20, 48, 75
proximity, 8, 23, 29, 33, 51, 75, 76, 88, 93
Psalms 12:4, 176; 91:15, 182
psyche, 22
Ptolemy, 178

representation, 4, 11, 13, 16, 20, 32, 33, 47, 58, 65,169
responsibility, 5, 22, 25, 27, 29, 30, 32, 33, 35–7, 75, 170
Revelation, 180
Rosenzweig, 51
Saint-Exupéry, 85, 88
Saying [Dire], 93
Schelling, 55
science, 91, 174
Scotus, Duns, 64

Seelisberg, 79, 80, 81
sefirot, 63
Sein und Zeit, 25
Septuagintal, 177
sociality, 8, 29, 30
Sollen, 50, 60
soul, 8, 16, 28, 64, 67, 75, 82, 91, 95
Spinoza, 55, 66, 68, 69, 74, 166
Stoics, 60
subjectivism, 176
Symposium, 10
synchrony, 12, 173
synthesis, passive, 20

Talmud, 177
there is, the 93
Thomas, St., 61, 64
Timaeus, 64
tiptoe, being-on-, 20
totalitarianism, 176
totality, 39
totality, 4, 39, 40–2, 44–7, 49, 51, 56, 58, 60, 70, 71; hermeneutic, 48
transcendence, 3, 5, 6, 7, 8, 11, 26, 31, 33, 35, 42, 50, 54, 55, 72, 95, 169, 170, 177
truth, 48, 54, 62

unhappy consciousness, 9, 84

Vanikoff, 82
vigilence, 5, 26, 32
violence, 23, 24, 25, 56, 169, 172, 177

Wahl, 93
Weil, (Eric), 175, 176
wisdom, 8, 9, 36, 72, 92,176

195

European Perspectives
A Series in Social Thought and Cultural Criticism
Lawrence D. Kritzman, Editor